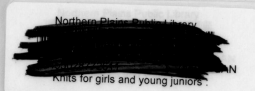
Knits

for GIRLS

and

YOUNG

JUNIORS

knits

for GIRLS
and
YOUNG
JUNIORS

17
CONTEMPORARY
DESIGNS
for Sizes 6 to 12

lee gant

**STACKPOLE
BOOKS**

Guilford, Connecticut

Published by Stackpole Books
An imprint of Globe Pequot
Trade Division of The Rowman & Littlefield Publishing Group, Inc.
4501 Forbes Boulevard, Suite 200, Lanham, Maryland 20706

Distributed by
NATIONAL BOOK NETWORK
800-462-6420

Photography: Jonathan Kirker Photography
Fashion Consultant and Styling Editor: Karissa Clark

We have made every effort to ensure the accuracy and completeness of these instructions. We cannot, however, be responsible for human error, typographical mistakes, or variations in individual work.

British Library Cataloguing in Publication Information Available

Library of Congress Cataloging-in-Publication Data
Names: Gant, Lee, author.
Title: Knits for girls and young juniors : 17 contemporary designs for sizes 6 to 12 / Lee Gant.
Description: Lanham : Stackpole Books, [2017] | Includes bibliographical references.
Identifiers: LCCN 2017014057 (print) | LCCN 2017018975 (ebook) | ISBN 9780811765787 (e-book) | ISBN 9780811715638 (paperback) | ISBN 9780811765787 (ebook)
Subjects: LCSH: Knitting--Patterns. | Knitwear. | Girls' clothing.
Classification: LCC TT825 (ebook) | LCC TT825 .G26 2017 (print) | DDC 746.43/2--dc23
LC record available at https://lccn.loc.gov/2017014057

♾™ The paper used in this publication meets the minimum requirements of American National Standard for Information Sciences—Permanence of Paper for Printed Library Materials, ANSI/NISO Z39.48-1992.

Printed in the United States of America

contents

preface

Girls just want to be girls. At the ocean, on the playground, in the park or out for a walk—looking good makes every girl happy.

Knitters just want to knit.

This unique collection of dresses, scarves, coats, and sweaters gives us all something to be happy about. Not all of the pieces will knit up in a hurry, so take your time, and enjoy the process. Be confident in your abilities, and in no time you and your girls will be looking good and feeling good in any of these special knits.

With love in every stitch,

Lee

acknowledgments

Thank you to my photographer, Jonathan Kirker, for finding so much beauty in our backyards of Sonoma County, and to my models, Hailie, Kayla, Karissa, Gabby, Gracie, Nicole, Emily, and Amber. I couldn't have done this without you. And thank you Pat Hellhake for your knitting expertise.

Introduction

One day while shopping at the mall with my teenage granddaughter, I looked around and saw inspiration hanging from every rack . . . a chance to rethink, restyle, and focus my attention on designing knits for a new generation. Trends and styles may change, but one thing remains constant: girls love clothes and fashion.

We, the parents and grandparents, have knit and designed for babies, toddlers, young children, and adults, but few and far between do we find patterns for older girls and young juniors.

Teens who want to learn to knit are hard-pressed to find patterns that suit their taste as well. Although some sweaters, jackets, hats, and scarves might interest a young knitter, they are usually photographed on older models. I believe that pictures play a big role in how we view knits and how we, or our intended recipients, think we might look in them.

All of the patterns in this book are written with easy-to-follow directions. If you can knit and purl, there isn't anything you can't make with a little help. Stitch counts are given on all of the patterns, but please don't worry if you're off a stitch or two—unless you're working on a lace pattern, where the numbers really do matter. For the experienced knitters who prefer not to seam, patterns can be adjusted to be worked in the round.

Not all of the patterns are quick to knit, but the mindlessness of the process will allow for enjoyable meditative thought or a good movie or book on tape while knitting. Not only will moms and grandmas enjoy knitting these fashions, but my hope is that the girls themselves will want to learn to knit so they can feel the satisfaction of creating their own stylish wardrobe. We all know the benefits of knitting, and *Knits for Girls and Young Juniors* will satisfy not only the numbers of teen knitters growing by leaps and bounds, but all of us knitters who are looking for something new to knit that our loved ones will wear.

If you have questions or need advice, please feel free to contact me at leegantknits.com. I'd love to help.

Sizing Information

Although measurements are similar in some places, the numbers for the Girls' sizes are calculated for a younger age, whereas the Young Juniors' sizing is for a taller girl, between 5'1" and 5'3", with a higher bust, a shorter back-to-waist length, and a larger hip measurement.

Choose whichever size best matches the girl's measurements around the bust, waist, and hips, as the length can be adjusted in the knitting. If your girl is not available to measure, note that the Girls sizes are similar to store-bought sizes, so you can select based on the typical size the girl wears. For older and taller girls, choose from Young Juniors sizes, but note that Young Juniors sizes are not the same as store-bought "Junior" sizes, so consider the measurements carefully when choosing a size. Not all patterns adhere to the numbers on this chart, as some are designed with more or less ease (check the finished measurements to help choose your size for each pattern based on fit), but use this as a general guide to help with choosing a size.

GIRLS SIZES				
Size	Chest	Waist	Hip	Height
6	24" / 61 cm	21" / 53.5 cm	25" / 63.5 cm	4'1" / 1.25 m
7	25½" / 65 cm	22½" / 57 cm	26½" / 67.5 cm	4'4" / 1.32 m
8	26" / 66 cm	23" / 58.5 cm	27" / 68.5 cm	4'6" / 1.37 m
10	28" / 71 cm	24" / 61 cm	31" / 78.5 cm	4'9" / 1.45 m
12	30" / 76 cm	25" / 63.5 cm	31" / 78.5 cm	5'0" / 1.52 m

YOUNG JUNIORS SIZES				
Size	Chest	Waist	Hip	Back-Waist Length
5/6	28" / 71 cm	22" / 56 cm	31" / 78.5 cm	13½" / 34.5 cm
7/8	29" / 73.5 cm	23" / 58.5 cm	32" / 81.5 cm	14" / 35.5 cm
9/10	30½" / 77.5 cm	24" / 61 cm	33½" / 85 cm	14½" / 37 cm
11/12	32" / 81.5 cm	25" / 63.5 cm	35" / 89 cm	15" / 38 cm

GALLERY

emily's blue dress

page 24

shepherds' plaid scarf

page 36

green apple dress
page 41

dotted swiss dress

page 46

pinwheel dress

page 51

white dress

page 55

rainbow dress

page 60

red coat

page 66

plaid skirt

page 75

black top

page 80

sparkle vest

page 83

classic coat

page 86

tweed poncho
page 94

sporty stripes dress
and jacket

page 99

hawaii dress

page 109

PATTERNS

emily's blue dress

Enjoy meditative knitting on this minimally shaped, ruffled, blue jean button-down dress. Textured little capped sleeves top off the summer feel. Try each ruffle in a different color to make it your own! Seed stitch borders can be pressed flat or left turned up for added texture as shown in the photos.

SIZES
Girls 6 (7, 8, 10, 12): Young Juniors 5/6 (7/8, 9/10, 11/12) *Instructions are written for size 6; all other sizes are in parentheses. Girls and Young Juniors sizes are separated with a colon. For ease in knitting, circle your size before beginning.*

FINISHED MEASUREMENTS
Chest: 24 (25, 26, 28, 30): 26 (28, 30, 32) in. / 61 (63.5, 66, 71, 76): 66 (71, 76, 81.5) cm

Waist: 21 (22, 23, 24, 25): 22 (24, 25, 26) in. / 53.5 (56, 58.5, 61, 63.5): 56 (61, 63.5, 66) cm

Skirt length from dropped waist: 11 (12, 12½, 12½, 13): 12½ (13, 14, 14½) in. / 28 (30.5, 32, 32, 33): 32 (33, 35.5, 37) cm

YARN
Brown Sheep Company Cotton Fine; 1.7 oz / 50 g each approx. 222 yd. / 203 m; 80% cotton, 20% merino wool
- 6 (6, 7, 7, 8): 6 (7, 8, 8) skeins #CF760 Emperor's Robe

MATERIALS
- Size US 3 / 3.25 mm 24 in. / 61 cm or longer circular needle *(or size to obtain gauge)*
- Tapestry needle (sharp yarn darner works best for tucking cotton ends)
- Waste yarn
- Extra needles for holding ruffles (smaller size okay)
- Ring-type marker
- 12 ⅝ in. / 1.5 cm buttons

GAUGE
26 sts and 32 rows to 4 in. / 10 cm in St st

STITCH GUIDE

Seed Stitch

Row 1: [K1, p1] repeat across.

Row 2: Knit the purls and purl the knits.

PATTERN NOTES

- Fronts and back are knitted from the bottom up, separately for strength and stability at the side seams.
- Cap sleeves are picked up and knitted flat from the shoulders down.
- See page 117 for instructions on how to work the three-needle bind-off.

DRESS BACK

First Ruffle

Cast on 182 (187, 197, 202, 214): 190 (197, 202, 214) sts.

Work 3 rows for border in Seed st as follows:

Row 1: [K1, p1] repeat across (on some sizes there will be 1 st rem; knit last st).

Row 2: Knit the purls and purl the knits.

Row 3: Repeat Row 2.

Change to St st and work until piece from beginning measures 4½ (4½, 5, 5, 5): 5½ (5½, 6, 6) in. / 11.5 (11.5, 12.5, 12.5, 12.5): 14 (14, 15, 15) cm. End having completed a WS row.

Next row (RS): Work decrease row for your size as follows:

Girls 6: [K3, k2tog] 36 times, k2tog [145 sts rem].

Girls 7: [K3, k2tog] 37 times, k2tog [149 sts rem].

Girls 8: [K3, k2tog] 39 times, k2tog [157 sts rem].

Girls 10: [K3, k2tog] 40 times, k2 [162 sts rem].

Girls 12: K9, [k3, k2tog] 39 times, k10 [175 sts rem].

Young jrs. 5/6: [K3, k2tog] 38 times [152 sts rem].

Young jrs. 7/8: [K3, k2tog] 39 times, k2tog [157 sts rem].

Young jrs. 9/10: [K3, k2tog] 40 times, k2 [162 sts rem].

Young jrs. 11/12: K9, [k3, k2tog] 39 times, k10 [175 sts rem].

Work even in St st for 3½ (3½, 4, 4½, 5): 4 (4½, 5, 5) in. / 9 (9, 10, 11.5, 12.5): 10 (11.5, 12.5, 12.5) cm (not including ruffle).

Cut yarn and place sts on a spare needle.

Second Ruffle

Cast on 146 (150, 158, 162, 175): 152 (158, 162, 175) sts.

Work 3 rows in Seed st.

Change to St st and work for 4 (4, 4½, 5, 5½): 4½ (5, 5½, 5½) in. / 10 (10, 11.5, 12.5, 14): 11.5 (12.5, 14, 14) cm. End having completed a WS row.

Next row (RS): Place ruffle right side up on top of stockinette section of first piece and knit together one st from each needle across (ruffle joined).

Next row (WS): Work decrease row for your size as follows:

Girls 6: [P2, p2tog] 36 times, p2 [110 sts rem].

Girls 7: [P2, p2tog] 37 times, p2tog [112 sts rem].

Girls 8: [P2, p2tog] 39 times, p2tog [118 sts rem].

Girls 10: [P2, p2tog] 40 times, p2 [122 sts rem].

Girls 12: P9, [p2, p2tog] 39 times, p10 [136 sts rem].

Young jrs. 5/6: [P2, p2tog] 38 times [114 sts rem].

Young jrs. 7/8: [P2, p2tog] 39 times, p2tog [118 sts rem].

Young jrs. 9/10: [P2, p2tog] 40 times, p2 [122 sts rem].

Young jrs. 11/12: P9, [p2, p2tog] 39 times, p10 [136 sts rem].

Change to St st and work for 3 (3, 3, 3, 3): 3 (3, 3, 3½) in. / 7.5 (7.5, 7.5, 7.5, 7.5): 7.5 (7.5, 7.5, 9) cm from this decrease. End having completed a WS row.

Place sts on a spare needle. Cut yarn.

Third Ruffle

Cast on 110 (112, 118, 122, 136): 114 (118, 122, 136) sts.
Work 3 rows in Seed st.

Change to St st and work for 3½ (3½, 3½, 3½, 3½): 3½ (3½, 3½, 4) in. / 9 (9, 9, 9, 9): 9 (9, 9, 10) cm. End having completed a WS row.

Next row (RS): Place ruffle right side up on top of stockinette section of last piece and knit together one st from each needle across (all ruffles joined).

Next row (WS): Work decrease row for your size as follows:

Girls 6: [P1, p2tog, p2tog] 22 times [66 sts rem].
Girls 7: [P1, p2tog] 37 times, p1 [75 sts rem].
Girls 8: [P1, p2tog] 39 times, p1 [79 sts rem].
Girls 10: [P1, p2tog] 40 times, p2 [82 sts rem].
Girls 12: P2, [p1, p2tog] 44 times, p2 [92 sts rem].
Young jrs. 5/6: P4, [p2, p3tog] 21 times, p5 [72 sts rem].
Young jrs. 7/8: [P1, p2tog] 39 times, p1 [79 sts rem].
Young jrs. 9/10: [P1, p2tog] 40 times, p2 [82 sts rem].
Young jrs. 11/12: P2, [p1, p2tog] 44 times, p2 [92 sts rem].

Next row: Knit, decreasing with a k2tog 0 (1, 1, 0, 0): 0 (1, 0, 0) sts [66 (74, 78, 82, 92): 72 (78, 82, 92) sts rem]*.

Waistband

Work in Moss st for 1 (1, 1, 1, 1½): 1 (1½, 1½, 1½) in. / 2.5 (2.5, 2.5, 2.5, 4): (2.5, 4, 4, 4) cm.

Change to St st and begin increases as follows:

Increase row on RS: K1, M1, knit to last st, M1, k1.
Increase row on WS: P1, M1, purl to last st, M1, p1.

Work increase row every 7th (10th, 11th, 9th, 12th): 8th (8th, 8th, 11th) row 5 (4, 4, 5, 4): 6 (6, 7, 5) times to 76 (82, 86, 92, 100): 84 (90, 96, 102) sts.

Work even if necessary until back measures 5½ (6, 6½, 7, 7½): 7½ (7½, 8½, 9) in. / 14 (15, 16.5, 18, 19): 19 (19, 21.5, 23) cm from beginning of Seed st (or desired length to underarm). End having completed a WS row.

Armhole Shaping

Bind off 6 sts at the beginning of the next 2 rows. Place a pin-type marker somewhere in the middle of the first bind-off row for ease in measuring armhole depth.

Next row (RS): K1, ssk, knit to last 3 sts, k2tog, k1.
Next row: Purl across.

Repeat last 2 rows 6 times more [50 (56, 60, 66, 74): 58 (64, 70, 76) sts rem].

Continue with no further decreases until armhole from beginning (here's where the marker comes in handy) measures 4 (4½, 4½, 5, 5): 4½ (4½, 5, 5) in. / 10 (11.5, 11.5, 12.5, 12.5): 11.5 (11.5, 12.5, 12.5) cm. End having completed a WS row.

Back Neck Shaping

Next row (RS): Work across 38 (44, 46, 50, 56): 44 (48, 52, 56) sts, then place last 26 (32, 32, 34, 38): 30 (32, 34, 36) sts *just worked* on a holder or waste yarn for back neck and continue across rem 12 (12, 14, 16, 18): 14 (16, 18, 20) sts for right shoulder.

Next row (WS): Purl across shoulder sts.
Next row (RS): K1, ssk, knit to end.
Next row: Purl.

Repeat last 2 rows once more [10 (10, 12, 14, 16): 12 (14, 16, 18) sts rem].

Work even if necessary until total armhole length is 4½ (5, 5, 5½, 5½): 5 (5, 5½, 5½) in. / 11.5 (12.5, 12.5, 14, 14): 12.5 (12.5, 14, 14) cm.

Place sts on a holder or waste yarn.

Left Shoulder Shaping

Join yarn at neck edge on WS and purl one row.

Next row (RS): Knit to last 3 sts, k2tog, k1.

Next row (WS): Purl.

Repeat last 2 rows once more [10 (10, 12, 14, 16): 12 (14, 16, 18) sts rem].

Work even if necessary until total armhole length is 4½ (5, 5, 5½, 5½): 5 (5, 5½, 5½) in. / 11.5 (12.5, 12.5, 14, 14): 12.5 (12.5, 14, 14) cm.

Place sts on a holder or waste yarn.

DRESS FRONT

Work same as for back to * (after third ruffle) [66 (74, 78, 82, 92): 72 (78, 82, 92) sts].

Divide for Fronts

RIGHT FRONT

Next row (WS): Work in Seed st across 30 (34, 36, 38, 43): 33 (36, 38, 43) sts, bind off 6 sts and continue in Seed st across rem sts. Turn and work on right front only as follows (place sts from other side on waste yarn and hold for later).

Next row (RS): Work Seed st until band measures same as for back, or 1 (1, 1, 1, 1½): 1 (1½, 1½, 1½) in. / 2.5 (2.5, 2.5, 2.5, 4): 2.5 (4, 4, 4) cm.

Change to St st and begin increases for right front:

Increase row on RS: Knit to last st, M1, k1.

Increase row on WS: P1, M1, purl to end.

Work increase row every 7th (10th, 10th, 9th, 11th): 8th (8th, 8th, 10th) row 6 (5, 5, 6, 5): 7 (7, 8, 7) times to 36 (39, 41, 44, 48): 40 (43, 46, 50) sts.

Work even if necessary until front measures 5½ (6, 6½, 7, 7½): 7½ (7½, 8½, 9) in. / 14 (15, 16.5, 18, 19): 19 (19, 21.5, 23) cm from end of Seed st (or desired length to underarm). End having completed a RS row.

Armhole Shaping

Next row (WS): Bind off 6 sts at the beginning of the row.

Next row (RS): Knit to last 3 sts, k2tog, k1.

Next row: Purl.

Repeat last 2 rows 6 times more [23 (26, 28, 31, 35): 27 (30, 33, 37) sts rem].

Work even if necessary until armhole measures 2½ (3, 3, 3½, 3½): 3 (3, 3½, 3½) in. / 6.5 (7.5, 7.5, 9, 9): 7.5 (7.5, 9, 9) cm. End having completed a WS row.

Neck Shaping

Next row (RS): Bind off 4 (5, 5, 6, 7): 4 (5, 6, 7) sts and continue across row.

Next row: Purl to last 3 sts, p2tog-tbl, p1.

Next row (RS): K1, ssk, knit to end.

Repeat last 2 rows until 10 (10, 12, 14, 16): 12 (14, 16, 18) sts rem.

Work even until total armhole length is 4½ (5, 5, 5½, 5½): 5 (5, 5½, 5½) in. / 11.5 (12.5, 12.5, 14, 14): 12.5 (12.5, 14, 14) cm.

Place sts on a holder or waste yarn.

LEFT FRONT

Place sts from waste yarn on needle, join new yarn from side edge and work Seed st until band measures same as for right front, or 1 (1, 1, 1, 1½): 1 (1½, 1½, 1½) in. / 2.5 (2.5, 2.5, 2.5, 4): 2.5 (4, 4, 4) cm.

Change to St st and begin increases:

Increase row on RS: K1, M1, knit to end.

Increase row on WS: Purl to last st, M1, p1.

Work increase row every 7th (10th, 10th, 9th, 11th): 8th (8th, 8th, 10th) row 6 (5, 5, 6, 5): 7 (7, 8, 7) times to 36 (39, 41, 44, 48): 40 (43, 46, 50) sts.

Work even if necessary until front measures 5½ (6, 6½, 7, 7½): 7½ (7½, 8½, 9) in. / 14 (15, 16.5, 18, 19): 19 (19, 21.5, 23) cm from end of Seed st (or desired length to underarm). End having completed a RS row.

Armhole Shaping

Next row (WS): Bind off 6 sts at the beginning of the row.

Next row (RS): Knit to last 3 sts, k2tog, k1.

Next row: Purl.

Repeat last 2 rows 6 times more [23 (26, 28, 31, 35): 27 (30, 33, 37) sts rem].

Work even if necessary until armhole measures 2½ (3, 3, 3½, 3½): 3 (3, 3½, 3½) in. / 6.5 (7.5, 7.5, 9, 9): 7.5 (7.5, 9, 9) cm. End having completed a RS row.

Neck Shaping

Next row (WS): Bind off 4 (5, 5, 6, 7): 4 (5, 6, 7) sts and continue across row.

Next row: Knit to last 3 sts, k2tog, k1.

Next row (WS): P1, p2tog, purl to end.

Repeat last 2 rows until 10 (10, 12, 14, 16): 12 (14, 16, 18) sts rem.

Work even until total armhole length is 4½ (5, 5, 5½, 5½): 5 (5, 5½, 5½) in. / 11.5 (12.5, 12.5, 14, 14): 12.5 (12.5, 14, 14) cm.

Use the three-needle bind-off to connect fronts to back at the shoulders from the WS.

BUTTON BAND

Begin at center front neck edge from the RS and pick up and knit 2 sts for every 3 rows to bind-off at waist. Count your sts and keep a note; you'll want to pick up the same amount on the other side.

Turn and work in Seed st for 7 rows.

Bind off on RS in pattern.

BUTTONHOLE BAND

Begin after bind-off at waist edge from RS and pick up 2 sts out of every 3 rows to neck edge, or same amount of sts as other side.

Begin on WS and work 3 rows in Seed st.

Now is the time to determine how many buttons you want and where you would like to put them. Hang pin-type markers on the needle, one a few sts from the neck edge and another a few sts from the waist-band, and the rest as evenly spaced as you can. Next, count the sts and adjust the markers so there is the same number of sts between them. It's okay if you're off by one st here and there. These markers will place your buttonholes.

Continue as follows:

Next row (RS): Maintaining Seed st pattern throughout row, work to first marker, *YO, remove marker and work 2 sts together, work to next marker and repeat from *. Continue making buttonholes in this manner to end of row.

Next row (WS): Work in Seed st, knitting or purling into the long side of the yarn overs (you want to make a hole here) across row.

Work 2 more rows in Seed st and bind off in pattern on RS.

SLEEVES

From the RS, pick up and knit 3 out of 4 sts around
    armhole edge.
Next row (WS): Work in Seed st to last 6 sts, w&t.
Next row (RS): Work to last 6 sts, w&t.
Next row (WS): Work in Seed st to last 10 sts, w&t.
Next row (RS): Work to last 10 sts, w&t.
Next row (WS): Work in Seed st to last 12 sts, w&t.
Next row (RS): Work to last 12 sts, w&t.
Continue as established, working 2 less sts each row
    until sleeve cap at shoulders measures 2 in. / 5 cm or
    desired length.
Work across last RS row and bind off in pattern on the
    WS.

COLLAR

From center front (not including buttonbands) on RS,
    pick up and knit 2 out of 3 sts around, knit all sts from
    holder at back neck, knit 2 out of 3 to other front.
Work 3½–4 in. / 9–10 cm in Seed st.
Bind off in pattern.

FINISHING

Stitch side and sleeve seams with mattress stitch from
    the RS.
Sew buttons opposite buttonholes.
Turn work inside out and stitch buttonband down at
    front, leaving several buttons free to open at neck
    edge as desired.
Weave in all ends and steam lightly or block according
    to directions on ball band.

cabled sweater

Fashioned with three traditional cables, this roomy Aran heirloom knit complements a favorite pair of jeans to keep warm on a chilly winter day. Easy bottom-up construction and sleeves knitted flat with no cap shaping make joining and finishing a breeze.

SIZES

All Girls sizes 6 (7, 8, 10, 12)
Instructions are written for size 6; all other sizes are in parentheses.

FINISHED MEASUREMENTS

Chest: 28 (30, 32, 34, 36) in. / 71 (76, 81.5, 86.5, 91.5) cm
Length: 17 (18½, 20, 21½, 22½) in. / 43 (47, 51, 54.5, 57) cm

YARN

Cascade Yarns 220 Superwash; 3.5 oz / 100 g each
  approx. 220 yd. / 203 m; 80% cotton, 20% merino
  wool
  • 5 (5, 6, 6, 6) skeins #862 Walnut Heather

MATERIALS

  • Size US 5 / 3.75 mm and US 6 / 4 mm needles
    (*or size to obtain gauge*)
  • Size US 5 / 3.75 mm 16 in. / 40.5 cm circular needle
    (*or desired needle for knitting in the round*)
  • Tapestry needle
  • Waste yarn
  • Cable needle
  • Pin-type stitch marker

GAUGE

20 sts and 28 rows to 4 in. / 10 cm in St st on size US 6 / 4 mm needles

STITCH GUIDE

C4B. Slip next 2 sts to CN and hold at back, k2, k2 from CN.

C4F. Slip next 2 sts to CN and hold at front, k2, k2 from CN.

T5BP. Slip next 3 sts to CN and hold at back, k2, then p1, k2 from CN.

T3B. Slip next st to CN and hold at back, k2, p1 from CN.

T3F. Slip next 2 sts to CN and hold at front, p1, k2 from CN.

Triangle Cable (over 17 sts)
Row 1 (RS): K2, p4, k2, p1, k2, p4, k2.
Row 2: K6, p2, k1, p2, k6.
Row 3: P6, T5BP, p6.
Row 4: Same as Row 2.
Row 5: P5, T3B, k1, T3F, p5.
Row 6: K5, p2, k1, p1, k1, p2, k5.
Row 7: P4, T3B, k1, p1, k1, T3F, p4.
Row 8: K4, p2, k1, [p1, k1] twice, p2, k4.
Row 9: P3, T3B, k1, [p1, k1] twice, T3F, p3.
Row 10: K3, p2, k1, [p1, k1] 3 times, p2, k3.
Row 11: P2, T3B, k1, [p1, k1] 3 times, T3F, p2.

Row 12: K2, p2, k1, [p1, k1] 4 times, p2, k2.
Row 13: P1, T3B, k1, [p1, k1] 4 times, T3F, p1.
Row 14: K1, p2, k1, [p1, k1] 5 times, p2, k1.
Row 15: T3B, k1, [p1, k1] 5 times, T3F.
Row 16: P2, k1, [p1, k1] 6 times, p2.
Repeat these 16 rows for pattern.

Honeycomb Cable (multiple of 8)
Row 1 (RS): Knit.
Row 2: Purl.
Row 3: [C4B, C4F] repeat to end.
Row 4: Purl.
Row 5: Same as Row 1.
Row 6: Same as Row 2.
Row 7: [C4F, C4B] repeat to end.
Row 8: Purl.
Repeat these 8 rows for pattern.

Braid Cable (over 9 sts)
Row 1 (RS): K4, p1, k4.
Row 2: P4, k1, p4.
Row 3: C4B, p1, C4F.
Row 4: P4, k1, p4.
Repeat these 4 rows for pattern.

BACK

With smaller needle, cast on 101 (107, 113, 119, 125) sts.

Next row (RS): [P2, k1b] repeat to last 2 sts, p2.

Next row (WS): [K2, p1] repeat to last 2 sts, k2.

Repeat last 2 rows until ribbing measures 1–2½ in. / 2.5–6.5 cm (or desired length), increasing 9 (11, 13, 13, 15) sts (by working into the front and back of same st) evenly spaced across last WS row [110 (118, 126, 132, 140) sts rem].

Change to larger needle.

Row 1 (RS): P3 (3, 3, 6, 6), work Row 1 of Braid Cable over next 9 sts, p2, k1b, p2, work Row 1 of Triangle Cable over next 17 sts, p2, k1b, p2, work Row 1 of Honeycomb Cable over next 32 (40, 48, 48, 56) sts, p2, k1b, p2, work Row 1 of Triangle Cable, p2, k1b, p2, work Row 1 of Braid Cable, p3 (3, 3, 6, 6).

Row 2 (WS): K3 (3, 3, 6, 6), work Row 2 of Braid Cable over next 9 sts, k2, p1, k2, work Row 2 of Triangle Cable over next 17 sts, k2, p1, k2, work Row 2 of Honeycomb Cable over next 32 (40, 48, 48, 56) sts, k2, p1, k2, work Row 2 of Triangle Cable, k2, p1, k2, work Row 2 of Braid Cable, k3 (3, 3, 6, 6).

Continue pattern as set until piece from the beginning measures 12 (13, 14, 15, 16) in. / 30.5 (33, 35.5, 38, 40.5) cm or desired length to armhole. End having completed a WS row.

Armhole Shaping

Bind off 3 (3, 6, 6, 6) sts at the beginning of the next 2 rows. Hang a pin-type marker somewhere in the middle of the first bind-off row for ease in measuring armhole depth.

Next row (RS): K1, ssk, work to last 3 sts, k2tog, k1.
Work WS row.
Repeat last 2 rows twice more [98 (106, 108, 114, 122) sts rem].*
Continue on these sts until armhole measures 4½ (5, 5½, 6, 6) in. / 11.5 (12.5, 14, 15, 15) cm.

Back Neck Shaping

Work across 65 (73, 76, 81, 89) sts, place last 32 (40, 44, 48, 56) sts *just worked* to a holder or waste yarn and continue across row.
Work one WS row across 33 (33, 32, 33, 33) shoulder sts only.
Next row (RS): K1, ssk, work in pattern to end.
Repeat last 2 rows once more to 31 (31, 30, 31, 31) sts. Place sts on a holder or waste yarn.
Join new yarn at neck edge on WS and work across left shoulder.
Next row (RS): Work in pattern to last 3 sts, k2tog, k1.
Work one WS row.
Repeat last 2 rows once more to 31 (31, 30, 31, 31) sts. Place sts on a holder or waste yarn.

FRONT

Work same as for back through armhole shaping to *.
Work until armhole measures 3 (3½, 4, 4½, 4½) in. / 7.5 (9, 10, 11.5, 11.5) cm. End having completed a WS row.

Front Neck Shaping

Work across 59 (67, 72, 75, 83) sts, place last 20 (28, 36, 36, 44) sts *just worked* on a holder or waste yarn and continue across row on rem 39 (39, 36, 39, 39) sts for right shoulder.
Work back on WS.
Next row (RS): K1, ssk, work in pattern to end.
Next row: Work in pattern to last 3 sts, p2tog-tbl, p1.
Work last 2 rows until 31 (31, 30, 31, 31) sts rem.
Continue if necessary, with no further decreases, until armhole measures 5 (5½, 6, 6½, 6½) in. / 12.5 (14, 15, 16.5, 16.5) cm or same as back. Place sts on a holder or waste yarn.
Join new yarn at neck edge on WS and work across in pattern.
Next row (RS): Work in pattern to last 3 sts, k2tog, k1.
Next row: P1, p2tog, work in pattern to end of row.
Work last 2 rows until 31 (31, 30, 31, 31) sts rem.

Continue if necessary, with no further decreases, until armhole measures 5 (5½, 6, 6½, 6½) in. / 12.5 (14, 15, 16.5, 16.5) cm or same as back.
With WS facing out, connect shoulders using the three-needle bind-off (see page 117).

SLEEVES (make two)

With smaller needles, cast on 56 (56, 59, 62, 62) sts.
Next row (RS): [P2, k1b] repeat to last 2 sts, p2.
Next row (WS): [K2, p1] repeat to last 2 sts, k2.
Repeat last 2 rows until ribbing measures 2–2½ in. / 5–6.5 cm or desired length, increasing 1 (1, 0, 1, 1) st (by working into the front and back of same st) evenly spaced across last WS row [57 (57, 59, 63, 63) sts rem].
Change to larger needles and continue as follows:
Row 1 (RS): P6 (6, 7, 9, 9), work Row 1 of Braid Cable over next 9 sts, p2, k1b, p2, work Row 1 of Triangle Cable over next 17 sts, p2, k1b, p2, work Row 1 of Braid Cable, p6 (6, 7, 9, 9).

number to a multiple of 3. Place a marker and continue in rnds as follows:

Rnd 1: [P2, k1b] repeat around.

Rnd 2: [P2, k1] repeat around.

Work Rnds 1 and 2 until collar measures 2½–3 in. / 6.5–7.5 cm or desired length. Bind off loosely in pattern, leaving a long tail. Fold collar to inside, if desired, and stitch down.

FINISHING

Position center of sleeve at shoulder and stitch into armhole, including bound-off area at underarm. Repeat for second sleeve.

Using mattress stitch from the RS, sew up side and sleeve seams.

Weave in any ends and steam lightly or block according to directions on ball band.

Row 2 (WS): K6 (6, 7, 9, 9), work Row 2 of Braid Cable over next 9 sts, k2, p1, k2, work Row 2 of Triangle Cable over next 17 sts, k2, p1, k2, work Row 2 of Braid Cable, k6 (6, 7, 9, 9).

These 2 rows set pattern. Work 10 (9, 8, 8, 8) rows, then work increase row as follows:

Increase row: Work 1 st, M1, work to last st, M1, work 1 st. (The RS will be purls and the WS will be knits.)

Work increase row every 11th (10th, 9th, 9th, 9th) row 7 (8, 9, 10, 10) times more to 73 (75, 79, 85, 85) sts.

Work even if necessary until sleeve from beginning measures 15 (15½, 16½, 17½, 18) in. / 38 (39.5, 42, 44.5, 45.5) cm or desired length to underarm. Bind off on RS in pattern.

Make other sleeve to match.

COLLAR

With smaller needle, begin at left front shoulder seam and pick up and knit 3 out of 4 sts around, including live sts from back and front neck holders. Adjust

two easy colorwork scarves

Shepherds' Plaid

Houndstooth

shepherds' plaid scarf

A beginner's introduction to Fair Isle knitting in the round, both this scarf and the following Hounds-tooth Scarf incorporate the same construction. With only a four- or six-row pattern repeat, either will be easy to memorize and whip up in a short amount of time. The tube construction allows for a thick and cozy scarf for any age. Pom-poms optional.

FINISHED MEASUREMENTS
Approx. 7 in. x 54 in. / 18 cm x 137 cm

YARN
Cascade Yarns Heritage 150; 5.3 oz / 150 g each approx. 492 yd. / 450 m; 75% merino wool, 25% nylon
- 1 skein #5640 Rust (Color A)
- 1 skein #5618 Cream (Color B)

MATERIALS
- Size US 4 / 3.5 mm 16 in. / 40.5 cm circular needle (*or size to obtain gauge*)
- Tapestry needle
- Ring-type marker
- Pom-pom maker (optional)

GAUGE
28 sts and 32 rows to 4 in. / 10 cm in pattern
Gauge is not crucial for this project.

PATTERN NOTES
- This scarf is knitted in the round, working a two-color Fair Isle pattern.
- See page 117 for instructions on how to work the three-needle bind-off.

SCARF

With Color A, Rust, cast on 100 sts; place a marker and
    join into a round, being careful not to twist sts. Join
    in Color B, Cream, and work from chart or as follows:
Rnd 1: [K1B, k1A] repeat around.
Rnd 2: [K1A, k1B] repeat around.
Rnd 3: [K1B, k3A, k1B, k1A, k3B, k1A] repeat around.
Rnd 4: [K5A, k5B] repeat around.
Rnd 5: [K1B, k3A, k1B, k1A, k3B, k1A] repeat around.
Rnd 6: [K1A, k1B] repeat around.
Rnd 7: [K1B, k1A] repeat around.
Rnd 8: [K1A, k3B, k1A, k1B, k3A, k1B] repeat around.
Rnd 9: [K5B, k5A] repeat around.
Rnd 10: [K1A, k3B, k1A, k1B, k3A, k1B] repeat around.
Repeat these 10 rnds for pattern.
Work as established until scarf measures 54 in. /
    137 cm or desired length.
Fold scarf at beginning of rnd and use the three-needle
    bind-off to connect 50 sts from each side together.
Fold scarf in same place at the other end (tail should
    mark your place) and whipstitch tube closed.

FINISHING

With remaining yarn, make and stitch pom-poms or
    tassels to corners, if desired.
Weave in ends.

SHEPHERDS' PLAID

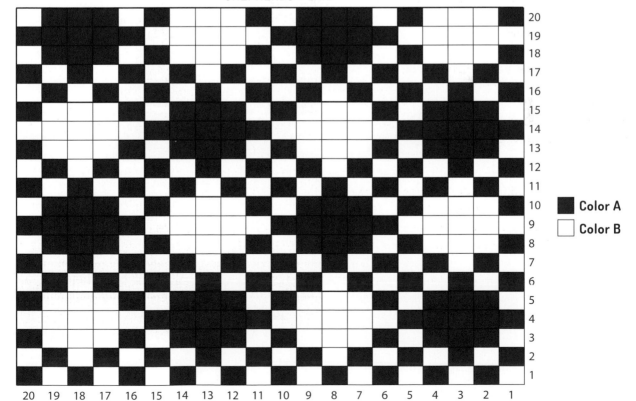

■ Color A
□ Color B

houndstooth scarf

The houndstooth pattern gives this scarf an air of subtle sophistication, but don't let the complicated look deceive you! It is just a four-round repeating colorwork pattern. This scarf is a great project for learning or practicing colorwork.

FINISHED MEASUREMENTS
Approx. 7 in. x 58 in. / 18 cm x 147 cm

YARN
Cascade Yarns Heritage 150; 5.3 oz / 150 g each approx. 492 yd. / 450 m; 75% merino wool, 25% nylon
- 1 skein #5609 Bark (Color A, dark brown)
- 1 skein #5610 Camel (Color B, light brown)

MATERIALS
- Size US 4 / 3.5 mm 16 in. / 40.5 cm circular needle (*or size to obtain gauge*)
- Tapestry needle
- Ring-type marker
- Pom-pom maker (optional)

GAUGE
28 sts and 32 rows to 4 in. / 10 cm in pattern
Gauge is not crucial for this project.

PATTERN NOTES
- This scarf is knitted in the round, working a two-color Fair Isle pattern.
- See page 117 for instructions on how to work the three-needle bind-off.

SCARF

With Color A, cast on 100 sts; place a marker and join
   into a round, being careful not to twist sts. Join in
   Color B and work from chart or as follows:

Rnd 1: K1A, [k1B, k3A] repeat to last 3 sts, k1A, k2B.

Rnd 2: [K1A, k3B] repeat around.

Rnd 3: [K3B, k1A] repeat around.

Rnd 4: K2A, [k1B, k3A] repeat to last 2 sts; k1B, k1A.

Repeat these 4 rnds for pattern.

Work as established until scarf measures 58 in. /
   147.5 cm.

Fold scarf at beginning of rnd and use the three-needle
   bind-off to connect 50 sts together.

Fold scarf in same place at other end (tail should mark
   your place) and whipstitch tube closed.

FINISHING

With remaining yarn, make and stitch 4 pom-poms or
   tassels to corners, if desired.

Weave in ends.

HOUNDSTOOTH

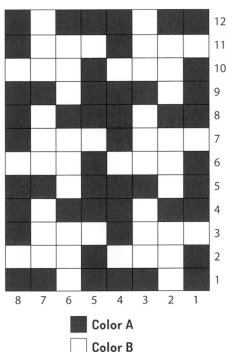

■ Color A
□ Color B

cute customizable dress: two versions

green apple dress

The construction for this dress and the following Dotted Swiss Dress are basically the same, although the Dotted Swiss incorporates a contrast color yarn every few rows. The dresses can be worked in the round or back and forth in rows; directions are given for both. Lace is knitted first, then stitches are picked up from the side edge of the lace to work the bottom tier of the dress. Make each layer in a different color, or mix and match layers and dots on either style.

SIZES

Girls 6 (7, 8, 10, 12): Young Juniors 5/6 (7/8, 9/10, 11/12)

Instructions are written for size 6; all other sizes are in parentheses. Girls and Young Juniors sizes are separated with a colon. For ease in knitting, circle your size before beginning.

FINISHED MEASUREMENTS

Chest: 24 (25, 26, 28, 30): 28 (29, 31, 32) in. / 61 (63.5, 66, 71, 76): 71 (73.5, 78.5, 81.5) cm

Waist: 21 (22, 23, 24, 25): 22 (23, 24, 25) in. / 53.5 (56, 58.5, 61, 63.5): 56 (58.5, 61, 63.5) cm

Total length: 25½ (27½, 29½. 31½, 33½): 27½ (29½, 31½, 33½) in. / 65 (70, 75, 80, 85): 70 (75, 80, 85) cm.

Note: If you want a shorter dress, simply decrease the length of first three tiers by the same amount.

YARN

Knit Picks Shine Sport; 1.7 oz / 50 g each approx. 110 yd. / 100 m; 60% pima cotton, 40% modal

- 2 (3, 3, 3, 3): 3 (3, 3, 3) skeins #9437 White (Contrast Color)
- 8 (9, 10, 11, 12): 9 (10, 11, 12) skeins #6561 Green Apple (Main Color)

MATERIALS

- Size US 3 / 3.25 mm 24 in. / 61 cm or longer circular needle (*or size to obtain gauge*)
- Size US 3 / 3.25 mm 16 in. / 40.5 cm circular needle (*or size to obtain gauge*)
- Size US 2 / 3 mm needles for lace edging (double-pointed needles work great)
- Blunt tapestry needle (for sewing seams)
- Sharp tapestry needle (for weaving in ends)
- Stitch holders or waste yarn
- 3 ring-type markers (if knitting in the round; see Pattern Note)
- 2 pin-type markers (optional)

GAUGE

24 sts and 32 rows to 4 in. / 10 cm in St st

STITCH GUIDE
Lace Edging
Cast on 8 sts.

Note: On all odd rows, slip the first st purlwise with yarn in front, then put yarn back between the two needles and proceed. To work a YO at the beginning of a row, either dip your needle under the working yarn before inserting into first 2 sts or insert needle into first 2 sts, then wrap yarn clockwise around right needle before finishing the k2tog.

Row 1 (WS): Sl1, k5, YO, k2.
Row 2: YO, k2tog, k7.
Row 3: Sl1, k4, YO, k2tog, YO, k2.
Row 4: YO, k2tog, k8.
Row 5: Sl1, k3, [YO, k2tog] twice, YO, k2.
Row 6: YO, k2tog, k9.
Row 7: Sl1, k2, [YO, k2tog] 3 times, YO, k2.
Row 8: YO, k2tog, k10.
Row 9: Sl1, k2, k2tog, [YO, k2tog] 3 times, k1.
Row 10: YO, k2tog, k9.
Row 11: Sl1, k3, k2tog, [YO, k2tog] twice, k1.
Row 12: YO, k2tog, k8.
Row 13: Sl1, k4, k2tog, YO, k2tog, k1.
Row 14: YO, k2tog, k7.
Row 15: Sl1, k5, k2tog, k1.
Row 16: YO, k2tog, k6.
Repeat these 16 rows for pattern.

Note: Each lace repeat of 16 rows yields 8 chain sts that you can easily count and will use to pick up the skirt.

PATTERN NOTE
• Directions are for knitting flat, but dress can be worked in the round, as described in Dotted Swiss Dress, then divided at armholes.

DRESS FRONT

Beginning with Contrast Color, White, and size US 2 needles, knit Lace Edging until you have 160 (168, 176, 184, 208): 184 (216, 232, 258) chain sts.

First Tier

With Main Color, Green Apple, from the RS, pick up and knit 160 (168, 176, 184, 208): 184 (216, 232, 258) sts through both loops of chain sts on top of lace edging.

Work in St st for 6 (6½, 7, 7½, 8): 6½ (7, 7½, 8) in. / 15 (16.5, 18, 19, 20.5): 16.5 (18, 19, 20.5) cm, not including lace. End having completed a WS row.

Decrease row (RS): Follow directions for your size:

Girls 6: K5, [k2tog, k3] 30 times, k5 [130 sts rem].

Girls 7: K4, [k2tog, k3] 32 times, k4 [136 sts rem].

Girls 8: K3, [k2tog, k3] 34 times, k3 [142 sts rem].

Girls 10: K7, [k2tog, k3] 34 times, k7 [150 sts rem].

Girls 12: K4, [k2tog, k3] 40 times, k4 [168 sts rem].

Young jrs. 5/6: K7, [k2tog, k3] 34 times, k7 [150 sts rem].

Young jrs. 7/8: [K8, k2tog] twice, k8, [k2tog, k2] 40 times, k8, [k2tog, k8] twice [172 sts rem].

Young jrs. 9/10: K1, [k2tog, k3] 46 times, k1 [186 sts rem].

Young jrs. 11/12: K9, [k2tog, k8] twice, [k2tog, k2] 50 times, [k2tog, k8] twice, k9 [204 sts rem].

Do not cut Main Color. Change to Contrast Color and knit one row. Cut Contrast Color.

Second Tier

With Main Color, work in St st for 6 (6½, 7, 7½, 8): 6½ (7, 7½, 8) in. / 15 (16.5, 18, 19, 20.5): 16.5 (18, 19, 20.5) cm. End having completed a WS row.

Decrease row (RS): Follow directions for your size:

Girls 6: K5, [k2tog, k2] 30 times, k5 [100 sts rem].

Girls 7: K8, [k2tog, k2] 30 times, k8 [106 sts rem].

Girls 8: K7, [k2tog, k2] 32 times, k7 [110 sts rem].

Girls 10: K9, k2tog, [k2, k2tog] 32 times, k2tog, k9 [116 sts rem].

Girls 12: K6, k2tog, [k2, k2tog] 38 times, k2tog, k6 [128 sts rem].

Young jrs. 5/6: K9, k2tog, [k2, k2tog] 32 times; k2tog, k9 [116 sts rem].

Young jrs. 7/8: [K2tog, k11] twice, [K2tog, k1] 40 times, [k2tog, k11] twice [128 sts rem].

Young jrs. 9/10: K1, [k2, k2tog] 46 times, k1 [140 sts rem].

Young jrs. 11/12: [K2tog, k8] 3 times, [k2tog, k1] 48 times, [k2tog, k8] 3 times [150 sts rem].

Do not cut Main Color. Change to Contrast Color and knit one row. Cut Contrast Color.

Third Tier

With Main Color, work in St st for 6 (6½, 7, 7½, 8): 6½ (7, 7½, 8) in. / 15 (16.5, 18, 19, 20.5): 16.5 (18, 19, 20.5) cm. End having completed a WS row.

Decrease row (RS): Follow directions for your size:

Girls 6: K8, [k2tog, k1] 28 times, k8 [72 sts rem].

Girls 7: K8, [k2tog, k1] 30 times, k8 [76 sts rem].

Girls 8: K7, [k2tog, k1] 32 times, k7 [78 sts rem].

Girls 10: K10, [k1, k2tog] 32 times, k10 [84 sts rem].

Girls 12: K7, [k2tog, k1] 38 times, k7 [90 sts rem].

Young jrs. 5/6: K10, [k1, k2tog] 32 times, k10 [84 sts rem].

Young jrs. 7/8: K1, [k2tog, k1] 42 times, k1 [86 sts rem].

Young jrs. 9/10: K1, [k2tog, k1] 46 times, k1 [94 sts rem].
Young jrs. 11/12: [K2tog, k1] 50 times [100 sts rem].
Do not cut Main Color. Change to Contrast Color and
knit one row. Cut Contrast Color.

Fourth Tier
With Main Color, work in St st for 1 (1½, 2, 2½, 2½): 1½
(2, 2, 2½) in. / 2.5 (4, 5, 6.5, 6.5): 4 (5, 5, 6.5) cm. End
having completed a WS row.
Note: If working in the round, divide for front and back
here; place half the amount of sts on a holder or
waste yarn and work in rows.

Armhole Shaping
Bind off 6 sts at the beginning of the next 2 rows. Hang
a pin-type marker somewhere in the middle of the
first bind-off row to aid in measuring the armhole
depth.
Next row (RS): K1, ssk, knit to last 3 sts, k2tog, k1.
Next row: Purl.
Repeat last 2 rows 2 times more [54 (58, 60, 66, 72): 66
(68, 76, 82) sts rem].
Work even on these sts until armhole measures 3 (3, 3,
3, 3½): 3 (3, 3½, 3½) in. / 7.5 (7.5, 7.5, 7.5, 9): 7.5 (7.5, 9,
9) cm. End having completed a WS row.

Neck Shaping
Work across 42 (45, 46, 51, 55): 51 (53, 59, 63) sts; place
last 30 (32, 32, 36, 38): 36 (38, 42, 44) sts *just worked*
from right needle to a holder or waste yarn for front
neck and continue across rem 12 (13, 14, 15, 17): 15
(15, 17, 19) sts.
Working on these sts only, turn and work as follows:
Next row (WS): Purl to last 3 sts, p2tog-tbl, p1.
Next row (RS): Knit.
Repeat last 2 rows twice more [9 (10, 11, 12, 14): 12 (12,
14, 15) sts rem].
Continue until total length of armhole measures 5 (5,
5, 5, 5½): 5 (5, 5½, 5½) in. / 12.5 (12.5, 12.5, 12.5, 14):
12.5 (12.5, 14, 14) cm. Place sts on holder or waste
yarn.

Join new yarn at neck edge on WS and purl across.
Next row (RS): Knit to last 3 sts, k2tog, k1.
Repeat last 2 rows twice more [9 (10, 11, 12, 14): 12 (12,
14, 15) sts rem].

Continue until total length of armhole measures 5 (5, 5,
5, 5½): 5 (5, 5½, 5½) in. / 12.5 (12.5, 12.5, 12.5, 14): 12.5
(12.5, 14, 14) cm. Place sts on holder or waste yarn.

DRESS BACK
Work same as for front until armholes measure 4 (4, 4,
4, 4½): 4 (4, 4½, 4½) in. / 10 (10, 10, 10, 11.5): 10 (10,
11.5, 11.5) cm. End having completed a WS row.

Back Neck Shaping
Work across 42 (45, 46, 51, 55): 51 (53, 59, 63) sts; place
last 30 (32, 32, 36, 38): 36 (38, 42, 44) sts *just worked*
from right needle to a holder or waste yarn for back
neck, and continue across rem 12 (13, 14, 15, 17): 15
(15, 17, 19) sts.
Working on these sts only, turn and work as follows:
Next row (WS): Purl to last 3 sts, p2tog-tbl, p1.
Next row (RS): Knit.

Repeat last 2 rows twice more [9 (10, 11, 12, 14): 12 (12, 14, 15) sts rem].
Work even if necessary until armhole measures same as front.
Place sts on a holder or waste yarn.

Join new yarn at neck edge on WS and purl across.
Next row (RS): Knit to last 3 sts, k2tog, k1.
Repeat last 2 rows twice more [9 (10, 11, 12, 14): 12 (12, 14, 15) sts rem].
Work even if necessary until armhole measures same as front.
With RS together, use the three-needle bind-off (see page 117) to connect the shoulders.

SLEEVE BORDERS (make two)

With Contrast Color, work Lace Edging to fit around armhole edge (try 9 scallops, or 72 chain sts).
Beginning at underarm, stitch into place. Stitch lace ends together.
Work same for other side.

NECK EDGE

With 16 in. / 40.5 cm circular needle and Contrast Color, begin just behind left shoulder and pick up and knit 3 out of 4 sts from neck edge, including all live sts from waste yarn at center front and center back.
Work 6 purl rnds and then bind off knitwise.
Whipstitch neck roll to inside.

FINISHING

Sew side seams using mattress stitch from the RS, stitch lace ends together at bottom of dress, and steam lightly or block according to directions on ball band.

dotted swiss dress

Following the same construction as the Green Apple Dress, the Dotted Swiss incorporates color changes and pretty dots, and directions given are for working in the round. Think of other ways you might customize this adorable dress style; the possibilities are endless!

SIZES

Girls 6 (7, 8, 10, 12): Young Juniors 5/6 (7/8, 9/10, 11/12)
Instructions are written for size 6; all other sizes are in parentheses. Girls and Young Juniors sizes are separated with a colon. For ease in knitting, circle your size before beginning.

FINISHED MEASUREMENTS

Chest: 24 (25, 26, 28, 30): 28 (29, 31, 32) in. / 61 (63.5, 66, 71, 76): 71 (73.5, 78.5, 81.5) cm

Waist: 21 (22, 23, 24, 25): 22 (23, 24, 25) in. / 53.5 (56, 58.5, 61, 63.5): 56 (58.5, 61, 63.5) cm

Total length: 25½ (27½, 29½. 31½, 33½): 27½ (29½, 31½, 33½) in. / 65 (70, 75, 80, 85): 70 (75, 80, 85) cm

YARN

Knit Picks Shine Sport; 1.7 oz / 50 g each approx. 110 yd. / 100 m; 60% pima cotton, 40% modal

- 5 (6, 7, 7, 8): 6 (7, 8, 9) skeins #9437 White (Color 1)
- 5 (5, 6, 6, 7): 6 (6, 7, 8) skeins #6557 Sky (Color 2)

MATERIALS

- Size US 3 / 3.25 mm 24 or 29 in. / 61 or 63.5 cm circular needle (*or size to obtain gauge*)
- Size US 2 / 3 mm needles for lace edging (double-pointed needles work great)
- Blunt tapestry needle (for sewing seams)
- Sharp tapestry needle (for weaving in ends)
- Stitch holders or waste yarn
- 3 ring-type markers
- 2 pin-type markers (optional)

GAUGE

24 sts and 32 rows to 4 in. /10 cm in St st

STITCH GUIDE

Lace Edging

Cast on 8 sts.

Note: On all odd rows, slip the first st purlwise with yarn in front, then put yarn back between the two needles and proceed. To work a YO at the beginning of a row, either dip your needle under the working yarn before inserting into first 2 sts or insert needle into first 2 sts, then wrap yarn clockwise around right needle before finishing the k2tog.

Row 1 (WS): Sl1, k5, YO, k2.

Row 2: YO, k2tog, k7.

Row 3: Sl1, k4, YO, k2tog, YO, k2.

Row 4: YO, k2tog, k8.

Row 5: Sl1, k3, [YO, k2tog] twice, YO, k2.

Row 6: YO, k2tog, k9.

Row 7: Sl1, k2, [YO, k2tog] 3 times, YO, k2.

Row 8: YO, k2tog, k10.

Row 9: Sl1, k2, k2tog, [YO, k2tog] 3 times, k1.

Row 10: YO, k2tog, k9.

Row 11: Sl1, k3, k2tog, [YO, k2tog] twice, k1.

Row 12: YO, k2tog, k8.

Row 13: Sl1, k4, k2tog, YO, k2tog, k1.

Row 14: YO, k2tog, k7.

Row 15: Sl1, k5, k2tog, k1.

Row 16: YO, k2tog, k6.

Repeat these 16 rows for pattern.

Note: Each lace repeat of 16 rows yields 8 chain sts that you can easily count and will use to pick up the skirt.

PATTERN NOTE

- Dress is worked in the round, then divided at armholes.

DRESS

Beginning with Color 1 (C1), White, and size US 2 needles, knit Lace Edging until you have 320 (336, 352, 368, 416): 368 (432, 464, 516) chain sts.

First Tier

With Color 2 (C2), Sky, from the RS, pick up and knit 320 (336, 352, 368, 416): 368 (432, 464, 516) sts through both loops of chains on top of lace edging (counts as Rnd 1). Place a marker being careful not to twist lace. This will be the center back.

Rnds 2, 3, and 4: Knit. On any of these rnds, place different color side markers as follows:

Girls 6: K80, PM, k160, PM, k80.

Girls 7: K84, PM, k168, PM, k84.

Girls 8: K88, PM, k176, PM, k88.

Girls 10: K92, PM, k184, PM, k92.

Girls 12: K104, PM, k208, PM, k104.

Young jrs. 5/6: K92, PM, k184, PM, k92.

Young jrs. 7/8: K108, PM, k216, PM, k108.

Young jrs. 9/10: K116, PM, k232, PM, k116.

Young jrs. 11/12: K129, PM, k258, PM, k129.

Rnd 5: [K3 C2, k1 C1] repeat around. Drop C1 but do not cut; carry up loosely behind work.

Rnds 6, 7, 8, and 9: Knit.

Rnd 10: K1 C2, [k1 C1, k3 C2] repeat around, end k2 C2.

Repeat Rnds 1–10 (Rnd 1 is a knit round) until piece (not including lace) measures 6 (6½, 7, 7½, 8): 6½ (7, 7½, 8) in. / 15 (16.5, 18, 19, 20.5): 16.5 (18, 19, 20.5) cm.

Remove beginning of rnd marker and knit to first side marker. This is now the new beginning of round.

Decrease rnd: Follow directions for your size:

Girls 6: *K5, [k2tog, k3] 30 times, k5; repeat from * [260 sts rem].

Girls 7: *K4, [k2tog, k3] 32 times, k4; repeat from * [272 sts rem].

Girls 8: *K3, [k2tog, k3] 34 times, k3; repeat from * [284 sts rem].

Girls 10: *K7, [k2tog, k3] 34 times, k7; repeat from * [300 sts rem].

Girls 12: *K4, [k2tog, k3] 40 times, k4; repeat from * [336 sts rem].

Young jrs. 5/6: *K7, [k2tog, k3] 34 times, k7; repeat from * [300 sts rem].

Young jrs. 7/8: *[K8, k2tog] twice, k8, [k2tog, k2] 40 times, k8, [k2tog, k8] twice; repeat from * [344 sts rem].

Young jrs. 9/10: *K1, [k2tog, k3] 46 times, k1; repeat from * [372 sts rem].

Young jrs. 11/12: *K9, [k2tog, k8] twice, [k2tog, k2] 50 times, [k2tog, k8] twice, k9; repeat from * [408 sts rem]. Do not cut C2 (Sky).

Second Tier

For this tier, switch Colors 1 and 2, using White as C2 and Sky as C1 for the one-stitch dots.

Work Rnds 1–10 as for first tier (*Note:* Do not move markers and don't worry if the dots don't line up over the first tier; the decreased sts will throw things off, but it'll look great) until second tier measures 6 (6½, 7, 7½, 8): 6½ (7, 7½, 8) in. / 15 (16.5, 18, 19, 20.5): 16.5 (18, 19, 20.5) cm.

Decrease rnd: Follow directions for your size:

Girls 6: *K5, [k2tog, k2] 30 times, k5; repeat from * [200 sts rem].

Girls 7: *K8, [k2tog, k2] 30 times, k8; repeat from * [212 sts rem].

Girls 8: *K7, [k2tog, k2] 32 times, k7; repeat from * [220 sts rem].

Girls 10: *K9, k2tog, [k2, k2tog] 32 times, k2tog, k9; repeat from * [232 sts rem].

Girls 12: *K6, k2tog, [k2, k2tog] 38 times, k2tog, k6; repeat from * [256 sts rem].

Young jrs. 5/6: *K9, k2tog, [k2, k2tog] 32 times, k2tog, k9; repeat from * [232 sts rem].

Young jrs. 7/8: *[K2tog, k11] twice, [K2tog, k1] 40 times, [k2tog, k11] twice; repeat from * [256 sts rem].

Young jrs. 9/10: *K1, [k2, k2tog] 46 times, k1; repeat from * [280 sts rem].

Young jrs. 11/12: *[K2tog, k8] 3 times, [k2tog, k1] 48 times, [k2tog, k8] 3 times; repeat from * [300 sts rem].

Do not cut C2 (White).

Third Tier

For this tier (same as first tier), White will be C1 and Sky will be C2.

Work Rnds 1–10 as for first tier (dots in white) until tier measures 6 (6½, 7, 7½, 8): 6½ (7, 7½, 8) in. / 15 (16.5, 18, 19, 20.5): 16.5 (18, 19, 20.5) cm.

Decrease rnd: Follow directions for your size:

Girls 6: *K8, [k2tog, k1] 28 times, k8; repeat from * [144 sts rem].

Girls 7: *K8, [k2tog, k1] 30 times, k8; repeat from * [152 sts rem].

Girls 8: *K7, [k2tog, k1] 32 times, k7; repeat from * [156 sts rem].

Girls 10: *K10, [k1, k2tog] 32 times, k10; repeat from * [168 sts rem].

Girls 12: *K7, [k2tog, k1] 38 times, k7; repeat from * [180 sts rem].

Young jrs. 5/6: *K10, [k1, k2tog] 32 times, k10; repeat from * [168 sts rem].

Young jrs. 7/8: *K1, [k2tog, k1] 42 times, k1; repeat from * [172 sts rem].

Young jrs. 9/10: *K1, [k2tog, k1] 46 times, k1; repeat from * [188 sts rem].

Young jrs. 11/12: *[K2tog, k1] 50 times, repeat from * [200 sts rem].

Fourth Tier

For the remainder of the dress, White will be C2 and Sky will be C1 for the one-stitch dots.

Work pattern as established for 1 (1½, 2, 2½, 2½): 1½ (2, 2, 2½) in. / 2.5 (4, 5, 6.5, 6.5): 4 (5, 5, 6.5) cm. End at second side marker.

Leave both yarns here and place next 72 (76, 78, 84, 90): 84 (86, 94, 100) sts on waste yarn or spare needle for bodice back (check to make sure this is the side where you first had the beginning of the rnd marker).

Armhole Shaping

Working on front sts only, begin with a purl row and bind off 6 sts at the beginning of the next 2 rows. Hang a pin-type marker somewhere in the middle of the first bind-off row to aid in measuring the armhole depth, continuing to work dots every 5th row as established.

Next row (WS): P1, p2tog-tbl, purl to last 3 sts, p2tog, p1.

Next row: Knit.

Repeat last 2 rows twice more [54 (58, 60, 66, 72): 66 (68, 76, 82) sts rem].

Work even on these sts until armhole measures 3 (3, 3, 3, 3½): 3 (3, 3½, 3½) in. / 7.5 (7.5, 7.5, 7.5, 9): 7.5 (7.5, 9, 9) cm. End having completed a WS row.

Neck Shaping

Work across 42 (45, 46, 51, 55): 51 (53, 59, 63) sts; place last 30 (32, 32, 36, 38): 36 (38, 42, 44) sts *just worked* from right needle to a holder or waste yarn for front neck and continue across rem 12 (13, 14, 15, 17): 15 (15, 17, 19) sts.

Working on these sts only, turn and work as follows:

Next row (WS): Purl to last 3 sts, p2tog-tbl, p1.

Next row (RS): Knit.

Repeat last 2 rows twice more [9 (10, 11, 12, 14): 12 (12, 14, 15) sts rem].

Continue until total length of armhole measures 5 (5, 5, 5, 5½): 5 (5, 5½, 5½) in. / 12.5 (12.5, 12.5, 12.5, 14): 12.5 (12.5, 14, 14) cm. Place sts on holder or waste yarn.

Join new yarn at neck edge on WS and purl across.

Next row (RS): Knit to last 3 sts, k2tog, k1.

Repeat last 2 rows twice more [9 (10, 11, 12, 14): 12 (12, 14, 15) sts rem].

Continue until total length of armhole measures 5 (5, 5, 5, 5½): 5 (5, 5½, 5½) in. / 12.5 (12.5, 12.5, 12.5, 14): 12.5 (12.5, 14, 14) cm. Place sts on holder or waste yarn.

Bodice Back

Place held sts on needle, join yarn and work same as for front until armholes measure 4 (4, 4, 4, 4½): 4 (4, 4½, 4½) in. / 10 (10, 10, 10, 11.5): 10 (10, 11.5, 11.5) cm. End having completed a WS row.

Back Neck Shaping

Work across 42 (45, 46, 51, 55): 51 (53, 59, 63) sts; place last 30 (32, 32, 36, 38): 36 (38, 42, 44) sts *just worked* from right needle to holder or waste yarn for back neck and continue across rem 12 (13, 14, 15, 17): 15 (15, 17, 19) sts.

Working on these sts only, turn and work as follows:

Next row (WS): Purl to last 3 sts, p2tog-tbl, p1.

Next row (RS): Knit across.

Repeat last 2 rows twice more [9 (10, 11, 12, 14): 12 (12, 14, 15) sts rem].

Work even if necessary until armhole measures same as front.

Place sts on holder or waste yarn.

Join new yarn at neck edge on WS and purl across.

Next row (RS): Knit to last 3 sts, k2tog, k1.

Repeat last 2 rows twice more [9 (10, 11, 12, 14): 12 (12, 14, 15) sts rem].

Work even if necessary until armhole measures same as front.

With RS together, use the three-needle bind-off (see page 117) to connect the shoulders together.

SLEEVE BORDERS

With White and smaller needles, work Lace Edging to fit around armhole edge (try 9 scallops, or 72 chains).

Begin at underarm and stitch into place. Stitch lace ends together.

Work same for other side.

NECK EDGE

With 16 in. / 40.5 circular needle and White, begin just behind left shoulder and pick up and knit 3 out of 4 sts from neck edge, including all live sts from waste yarn at center front and center back.

Work 6 purl rnds and then bind off knitwise.

Whipstitch neck roll to inside, if desired.

FINISHING

Sew lace seam at back cast-on edge and steam lightly or block according to directions on ball band.

pinwheel dress

Short-row construction and side-to-side knitting give this skirt its unique striped look. The bodice is picked up and knitted from the side of skirt. The sleeves and neck border are finished with attached I-cord.

SIZES
3/6 months (12 months, 18 months, 2T) (3T, 4T, 5T) (6, 6X, 7/8) 10/12
Instructions are written for size 3/6 months; all other sizes are in parentheses. Note: *This pattern has an extended size range for younger girls!*

FINISHED MEASUREMENTS
Chest: 20 (21, 22, 23) (24, 25, 26) (27, 28, 29) 30 in. / 51 (53.5, 56, 58.5) (61, 63.5, 66) (68.5, 71, 73.5) 76 cm
Length: 16 (17, 18, 19) (20, 21, 22½) (23½, 25, 27) 28 in. / 40.5 (43, 45.5, 48) (51, 53.5, 57) (59.5, 63.5, 68.5) 71 cm

YARN
Cascade Yarns Ultra Pima; 3.5 oz / 100 g each approx. 220 yd. / 200 m; 100% pima cotton
- 1 (1, 1, 2) (2, 2, 2) (2, 3, 3) 3 skeins #3728 White (Main Color)
- 1 skein #3773 Sky Blue (A)
- 1 skein #3711 China Pink (B)
- 1 skein #3758 Pale Seafoam (C)
- 1 skein #3757 Dark Seafoam (D)

MATERIALS
- Size US 4 / 3.5 mm 16 in. / 40.5 cm circular needle (*or size to obtain gauge*)
- Size US 4 / 3.5 mm 24 in. / 40.5 cm circular needle (*or size to obtain gauge*)
- Tapestry needle (sharp yarn darner works best for tucking cotton ends)
- Waste yarn
- Stitch markers

GAUGE
26 sts and 32 rows to 4 in. / 10 cm in St st

PATTERN NOTE

- Skirt is worked sideways in one piece with easy short-row shaping. Body is picked up and worked in the round, front and back worked separately at armholes, with three-needle bind-off at shoulders. Pick up sts from armhole and neck edges and finish with I-cord bind-off. See page 117 for instructions.

SKIRT

Note: When picking up wraps, insert needle into the wrap first, then knit it together with the stitch on the left needle. Color sequence is 4 rows each A, C, B, D, with 4-stitch differential undulating white short row in-between. Where yarn cuts, leave a tail long enough to weave in.

With Color A, cast on 60 (62, 66, 70) (74, 78, 82) (86, 92, 98) 104 sts.
Begin short row shaping as follows:
Row 1 (WS): With A, purl, do not cut yarn.

Row 2: Change to white and knit 45 (47, 50, 53) (56, 59, 61) (65, 69, 74) 78 sts, w&t, purl back (never cut white, but carry alongside edge).

Row 3: With A, knit to end, picking up wrap.

Row 4: Purl A, cut yarn.

Row 5: With white, knit 41 (43, 46, 49) (52, 55, 57) (61, 65, 69) 74, w&t, purl back.

Row 6: With C, knit to end, picking up wrap.

Row 7 (WS): With C, purl, do not cut yarn.

Row 8: With white, knit 37 (39, 42, 45 (48, 51, 53) (57, 61, 65) 70, w&t, purl back.

Row 9: With C, knit to end, picking up wrap.

Row 10: Purl C, cut yarn.

Row 11: With white, knit 33 (35, 38, 41) (44, 47, 49) (53, 57, 61) 66, w&t, purl back.

Row 12: With B, knit to end, picking up wrap.

Row 13: With B, purl, don't cut.

Row 14: With white, knit 29 (31, 34, 37) (40, 43, 45) (49, 53, 57) 62, w&t, purl back.

Row 15: With B, knit to end, picking up wrap.

Row 16: Purl B, cut yarn.

Row 17: With white, knit 25 (27, 30, 33) (36, 39, 41) (45, 49, 53) 58, w&t, purl back.

Row 18: With D, knit to end, picking up wrap.

Row 19: Purl with D, don't cut.

Row 20: With white, knit 25 (27, 30, 33) (36, 39, 41) (45, 49, 53) 58, w&t, purl back.

Row 21: With D, knit to end, picking up wrap.

Row 22: Purl D, cut yarn.

Row 23: With white, knit 29 (31, 34, 37) (40, 43, 45) (49, 53, 57) 62, w&t, purl back.

Row 24: With A, knit to end, picking up wrap.

Row 25: Purl A, don't cut.

Row 26: With white, knit 33 (35, 38, 41) (44, 47, 49) (53, 57, 61) 66, w&t, purl back.

Row 27: With A, knit to end, picking up wrap.

Row 28: Purl A, cut yarn.

Row 29: With white, knit 37 (39, 42, 45) (48, 51, 53) (57, 61, 65) 70, w&t, purl back.

Row 30: With C, knit to end, picking up wrap.

Row 31: Purl C, don't cut.

Row 32: With white, knit 41 (43, 46, 49) (52, 55, 57) (61, 65, 69) 74, w&t, purl back.

Row 33: With C, knit to end, picking up wrap.

Row 34 (WS): Purl C, cut yarn.

Row 35: With white, knit 45 (47, 50, 53) (56, 59, 61) (65, 69, 74) 78, w&t, purl back.

Row 36: With B, knit to end, picking up wrap.

Row 37: Purl B, do not cut.

Row 38: With white, knit 41 (43, 46, 49) (52, 55, 57) (61, 65, 69) 74, w&t, purl back.

Row 39: With B, knit to end, picking up wrap.

Row 40: Purl B, cut yarn.

Row 41: With white, knit 37 (39, 42, 45) (48, 51, 53) (57, 61, 65) 70, w&t, purl back.

Row 42: With D, knit to end, picking up wrap.

Row 43: Purl D, don't cut.

Row 44: With white, knit 33 (35, 38, 41) (44, 47, 49) (53, 57, 61) 66, w&t, purl back.

Row 45: With D, knit to end, picking up wrap.

Row 46: Purl D, cut yarn.

Row 47: With white, knit 29 (31, 34, 37) (40, 43, 45) (49, 53, 57) 62, w&t, purl back.

Row 48: With A, knit to end, picking up wrap.

Row 49: Purl A, don't cut.

Row 50: With white, knit 25 (27, 30, 33) (36, 39, 41) (45, 49, 53) 58, w&t, purl back.

Row 51: With A, knit to end, picking up wrap.

Row 52: Purl A, cut yarn.

Continue working pattern as established, keeping color sequence in 4 rows at waistband, with 4-stitch differential every white short row until waistband at the narrow end (no white here) has 40 (42, 44, 46) (48, 50, 52) (54, 56, 58) 60 [4-row] color changes.

Join skirt into a circle by either binding off and stitching sides together or picking up sts from the cast-on edge and using the three-needle bind-off (from the WS).

With MC, beginning at center back, from the RS, pick up and knit 3 out of every 4 sts across color bars of waistband to 120 (126, 132, 138) (144, 150, 156) (162, 168, 174) 180 sts. Place a marker and join into a round.

Knit 30 (31, 33, 34) (36, 38, 39) (41, 42, 44) 45 sts, place different color marker for side seam, knit 60 (64, 66, 70) (72, 74, 78) (80, 84, 86) 90 sts, place marker, knit to beginning marker at center back.

Knit in the round for 3 in. / 7.5 cm (or desired length to underarm), ending at side marker.

Divide for armholes: Knit across 60 (64, 66, 70) (72, 74, 78) (80, 84, 86) 90 sts and place them on a holder or waste yarn and set aside for front.

BACK

Note: Begin working back and forth in rows.

Bind off 6 sts at the beginning of the next 2 rows (bind off in purl on the WS).

Begin stripe pattern: 4 rows Color D, 2 rows MC, 4 rows Color A, 2 rows MC, 4 rows Color C, 2 rows MC, 4 rows Color B, 2 rows MC.

Continue in stripes and work even until bodice from armhole bind-off measures 3½ (4, 4½, 5) (5, 5½, 6½) (7, 7½, 8) 8½ in. / 9 (10, 11.5, 12.5) (12.5, 14, 16.5) (18, 19, 20.5) 21.5 cm. End having completed a WS row.

Back Neck Shaping

Next row (RS): Work across 33 (34, 37, 38) (41, 44, 46) (49, 51, 54) 55 sts, place last 18 (18, 20, 20) (22, 24, 26) (28, 30, 32) 32 sts *just worked* on holder or waste yarn for center neck, and work to end of row.

Next row: Purl.

5½, 6) 6 in. / 7.5 (7.5, 7.5, 9) (9, 10, 11.5) (12.5, 14, 15) 15 cm. End having completed a WS row.

Front Neck Shaping
Next row (RS): Work across 30 (33, 34, 37) (38, 39, 43) (44, 48, 49) 50 sts, place last 12 (14, 14, 16) (16, 16, 20) (20, 24, 24) 26 sts *just worked* on a holder or waste yarn for center neck, and work to end of row.
Next row: Purl.
Next row (RS): K1, ssk, knit to end.
Repeat last 2 rows 5 times more to 12 (13, 14, 15) (16, 17, 17) (18, 18, 19) 20 sts.
Work even if necessary until piece measures same as back, place sts on a holder or waste yarn.
Join new yarn to WS at neck edge and purl across.
Next row (RS): Knit to last 3 sts, k2tog, k1.
Next row: Purl.
Repeat last 2 rows 5 times more to 12 (13, 14, 15) (16, 17, 17) (18, 18, 19) 20 sts.
Work even if necessary until piece measures same as back.
Use the three-needle bind-off to connect the shoulder sts together from the wrong side.

ARMHOLE EDGING

Beginning at underarm, from the RS with 16 in. / 40.5 cm needle and MC, pick up and knit 3 out of 4 sts around armhole. Turn work and cast on 3 sts.
[K2, ssk, slip 3 sts to left needle] repeat around for I-cord bind-off.
Bind off and stitch cord ends together at underarm.
Repeat on other armhole.

NECK BORDER

Begin at center back and work same as for armholes.

FINISHING

Sew side and underarm seams, weave in all ends, and steam lightly or block according to directions on ball band.

Next row (RS): K1, ssk, knit to end.
Repeat last 2 rows twice more to 12 (13, 14, 15) (16, 17, 17) (18, 18, 19) 20 sts. Place on a holder or waste yarn.
Join new yarn to WS at neck edge and purl across.
Next row (RS): Knit to last 3 sts, k2tog, k1.
Next row: Purl.
Repeat last 2 rows twice more to 12 (13, 14, 15) (16, 17, 17) (18, 18, 19) 20 sts. Place on a holder or waste yarn.

FRONT

Place sts from holder on needle and work same as for back (including bind-offs for armhole).
Continue in stripes and work even until bodice from armhole bind-off measures 3 (3, 3, 3½) (3½, 4, 4½) (5,

white dress

An easy lace repeat for the bottom border, sleek shaping, and I-cord detail make this a special occasion dress for any young girl's graduation, or a teenager's party or a simple walk on the beach. Lace sleeves add a touch of elegance, but they can be omitted for the knitter not yet ready to incorporate decreases into a lace pattern. I say give it a try; the reward will be well worth it!

SIZES
Girls 6 (7, 8, 10, 12): Young Juniors 5/6 (7/8, 9/10, 11/12)
Instructions are written for size 6; all other sizes are in parentheses. Girls and Young Juniors sizes are separated with a colon. For ease in knitting, circle your size before beginning.

FINISHED MEASUREMENTS
Chest: 25 (26, 27, 28, 30): 28 (30, 31, 32) in. / 63.5 (66, 68.5, 71, 76): 71 (76, 78.5, 81.5) cm
Waist: 22½ (23, 24, 24½, 25): 22 (23, 24, 25) in. / 57 (58.5, 61, 62, 63.5): 56 (58.5, 61, 63.5) cm
Total length: 28 (29, 30, 32, 34): 33 (34, 36, 38) in. / 71 (73.5, 76, 81.5, 86.5): 84 (86.5, 91.5, 96.5) cm

YARN
Cascade Yarns Heritage 150; 5.3 oz. / 150 g each approx. 492 yd. / 450 m; 75% merino wool, 25% nylon
- 3 skeins #5682 White

MATERIALS
- Size US 5 / 3.75 mm 24 in. / 61 cm circular needle (*or size to obtain gauge*)
- Size US 5 / 3.75 mm 16 in. / 40.5 cm circular needle
- Size US 5 / 3.75 mm double-pointed needles
- Tapestry needle
- Waste yarn
- Ring-type markers, two colors

GAUGE
26 sts and 32 rows to 4 in. / 10 cm in St st

PATTERN NOTES

- Dress is worked from the bottom up in the round to armholes, then back and front are divided and worked separately. The three-needle bind-off (see page 117) is used at the shoulders, and sleeves are picked up and worked in the round.
- See page 117 for instructions on how to work the I-cord cast-on and I-cord bind-off.

DRESS

Using I-cord cast-on, make 176 (176, 184, 192, 201): 184 (192, 200, 208) sts. Place marker and join into the round, being careful not to twist I-cord. This will be the back of the dress, and the beginning of the round.

Begin Lace Pattern (multiple of 8, worked in the round) as follows:

Rnd 1: *Ssk [k1, YO] twice, k1, k2tog, k1; repeat from * around.

Rnds 2, 4, and 6: Knit.

Rnd 3: *Ssk, YO, k3, YO, k2tog, k1; repeat from * around.

Rnd 5: *YO, k1, k2tog, k1, ssk, k1, YO, k1; repeat from * around.

Rnd 7: *K1, YO, k2tog, k1, ssk, YO, k2; repeat from * around.

Rnd 8: Knit.

Work Rnds 1–8 three times more.

Change to St st (knit every round) and work until piece measures 6 in. / 15 cm from beginning.

Place side markers as follows (these side markers are essential): Knit 44 (44, 46, 48, 50): 46 (48, 50, 52), PM, knit 88 (88, 92, 96, 100): 92 (96, 100, 104) for front, PM, and continue to beginning of rnd (ending at center back).

Decrease rnd: *Knit to within 3 sts of side marker, k2tog, k1, SM, k1, ssk; repeat from *once more at other side marker and knit to end of rnd.

Work a decrease rnd every 9th (10th, 9th, 9th, 8th): 8th (8th, 9th, 9th) rnd 10 (9, 10, 11, 12): 13 (14, 14, 15) times total [136 (140, 144, 148, 152): 132 (136, 144, 148) sts rem].

Work even if necessary until piece from beginning measures approx. 13½ (13½, 13½, 14, 15): 15 (16½, 17½, 19) in. / 34 (34, 34, 35.5, 38): 38 (42, 44.5, 48.5) cm (or desired length to waist).

Increase rnd: *Knit to within 1 st of side marker, M1, k1, SM, k1, M1; repeat from * once more at other side marker and knit to end of rnd.

Work an increase rnd every 11th (13th, 14th, 12th, 10th): 5th (5th, 6th, 7th) rnd 4 (4, 4, 5, 7): 9 (11, 10, 11) times total [152 (156, 160, 168, 180): 168 (180, 184, 192) sts rem].

Work even if necessary until piece from waist measures approx. 5½ (6½, 7, 8, 9): 6 (7, 7½, 8) in. / 14 (16.5, 18, 20.5, 23): 15 (18, 19, 20.5) cm, or desired length to underarm.

Divide for front and back as follows: Knit to second side marker, then slip all front sts just worked to waste yarn or spare circular needle for holding, continue around to beginning of round, remove marker, and continue knitting across to end of row. You should have 76 (78, 80, 84, 90): 84 (90, 92, 96) sts on working needle (for back) and the same amount on hold for front.

BACK
Armhole Shaping
Begin working in St st in rows on back sts only.

Bind off 3 (3, 3, 4, 5): 5 (5, 4, 4) sts at the beginning of the next 2 rows. Helpful hint: Place a hanging marker somewhere in the middle of the first row to aid in the counting of rows, to ensure that the front and back are the same length.

Decrease row (WS): P1, p2tog-tbl, purl to last 3 sts, p2tog, p1.

Next row (RS): Knit.

Repeat last 2 rows 2 (2, 0, 1, 3): 3 (3, 1, 2) times more to 64 (66, 72, 72, 72): 66 (72, 80, 82) sts.

Work even with no further decreases until piece from armhole shaping measures 2½ in. / 6.5 cm. End having completed a WS row.

Work I-cord bind-off and fasten off.

With new yarn, from the RS, bend I-cord forward and pick up and knit into each st across in the row below and behind cord.

Next row: Purl across, decreasing or adding one st at edge so that your total number of sts equals 65 (65, 73, 73, 73): 65 (73, 81, 81). We will begin the Lace Pattern next, which must be a multiple of 8+1.

Begin Lace Pattern as follows:

Row 1: K1,*ssk, [k1, YO] twice, k1, k2tog, k1; repeat from *.

Rows 2, 4, and 6: Purl.

Row 3: K1,*ssk, YO, k3, YO, k2tog, k1; repeat from *.

Row 5: K1,*YO, k1, k2tog, k1, ssk, k1, YO, k1; repeat from *.

Row 7: K1,*k1, YO, k2tog, k1, ssk, YO, k2; repeat from *.

Row 8: Purl.

Work Rows 1–8 until lace (from I-cord) measures 2½ (3½, 3½, 4, 4½): 2½ (3½, 4, 4) in. / 6.5 (9, 9, 10, 11.5): 6.5 (9, 10, 10) cm. End having completed a WS row.

Place 14 (14, 16, 16, 16): 14 (16, 18, 18) sts on holder or waste yarn for shoulder, then place center 37 (37, 41, 41, 41): 37 (41, 45, 45) sts on a separate holder for neck, and rem 14 (14, 16, 16, 16): 14 (16, 18, 18) sts on a holder or waste yarn for other shoulder.

FRONT

Beginning on WS, join yarn and work armhole shaping, I-cord, and Lace Pattern same as for back. End having worked a WS row.

Use the three-needle bind-off to connect shoulder stitches together.

Place all live sts from front and back neck on a circular needle. Beginning at shoulder seam, join new yarn and work I-cord bind-off. Stitch cord ends together.

SLEEVES

Beginning at underarm, from the RS, pick up and knit 60 (72, 78, 78, 84): 60 (72, 78, 84) sts (try pick up 2, skip 1). PM for beginning of round, then knit 6 (8, 7, 7, 10): 10 (12, 7, 10) sts, place a different color marker, work Row 1 of Lace Pattern for Sleeves (see page 59) over next 48 (56, 64, 64, 64): 40 (48, 64, 64) sts, knit to last 6 (8, 7, 7, 10): 10 (12, 7, 10) sts, PM, w&t, purl back to first different color marker, w&t.

Working back and forth in rows, continue working each row of Lace Pattern for Sleeves while picking up wrap on st before w&t until short rows meet at beginning-of-the-round marker. You should still have the original number of picked up sts (lace pattern between markers and St sts at underarm) and a beautiful little shaped cap for the start of your sleeve. Proceed working in the round as follows:

Decrease rnd: K2tog, work to last 2 sts, ssk.

Hint: After decreasing all St sts away, place a marker every 8-st repeat nearest beginning and end of round to keep lace pattern correct on less than the 8-st repeat.

Work a decrease rnd every 7th (6th, 5th, 5th, 5th): 7th (6th, 5th, 5th) rnd 13 (16, 19, 19, 21): 13 (16, 19, 21) times to 35 (41, 41, 41, 43): 35 (41, 41, 43) sts.

Work even if necessary until sleeve measures 11½ (12, 12½, 13, 13½): 11½ (12, 13, 13½) in. / 29 (30.5, 32, 33, 34.5): 29 (30.5, 33, 34.5) cm, or desired length from underarm. End having completed a WS round.

Work I-cord bind-off *loosely*; stitch ends together.

Lace Pattern for Sleeves (multiple of 8):

Note: When sleeves are joined after short-row shaping, the even-numbered purl rows become knit rnds.

Row or Rnd 1: *Ssk, [k1, YO] twice, k1, k2tog, k1; repeat from * around.

Rows or Rnds 2, 4, and 6: Purl if working in rows, knit if working in rnds.

Row or Rnd 3: *Ssk, YO, k3, YO, k2tog, k1; repeat from * around.

Row or Rnd 5: *YO, k1, k2tog, k1, ssk, k1, YO, k1; repeat from * around.

Row or Rnd 7: * K1, YO, k2tog, k1, ssk, YO, k2; repeat from * around.

Row or Rnd 8: Purl if working in rows, knit if working in rnds.

FINISHING

Weave in all ends.
Block according to directions on ball band.

rainbow dress

Worked entirely in twisted rib, this is not a quick knit, but the addition of intarsia panels gives you something to keep you going. Easy construction with decorative buttons makes this one as much fun to wear as it is to knit.

SIZES
Girls 6 (7, 8, 10, 12); Young Juniors 5/6 (7/8, 9/10, 11/12)
Instructions are written for size 6; all other sizes follow. Girls and Young Juniors sizes are separated with a colon. For ease in knitting, circle your size before beginning.

FINISHED MEASUREMENTS
Chest: 24 (25, 26, 28, 30): 26 (28, 30, 31) in. / 61 (63.5, 66, 71, 76): 66 (71, 76, 78.5) cm

Waist/midriff: 22½ (23½, 24½, 25½, 26½): 23½ (25½, 26½, 27½) in. / 57 (59.5, 62, 65, 67.5): 59.5 (65, 67.5, 70) cm

YARN
Cascade Yarns 220 Superwash; 3.5 oz. / 100 g each approx. 220 yd. / 200 m; 100% superwash wool
• 5 (5, 6, 6, 7): 5 (6, 6, 7) skeins #1946 Dolphin (Gray)

Ella Rae Cozy Soft; 3.5 oz. / 100 g each approx. 213 yd. / 195 m; 25% superwash wool, 75% acrylic
• 1 skein #27 Medium Mint (Green)
• 1 skein #11 Bright Blue (Blue)
• 1 skein #13 Lavender (Purple)
• 1 skein #39 Bubble Gum Pink (Pink)
• 1 skein #30 Pink Coral (Dark Pink)
• 1 skein #25 Tangerine (Orange)
• 1 skein #26 Sunflower (Yellow)

MATERIALS
• Size US 6 / 4 mm 36–40 in. / 91.5–101.5 cm long circular needle (*or size to obtain gauge*)
• Size US 6 / 4 mm 16 in. / 40.5 cm circular needle
• Size US 6 / 4 mm double-pointed needles (*or any preferred needles for knitting in the round*)
• Tapestry needle
• Waste yarn
• Decorative buttons, optional

GAUGE

30 sts and 30 rows to 4 in. / 10 cm in double twisted rib

Note: Although worked in worsted weight yarn and size 6 needles, this produces a lovely corded rib at 7½ sts per inch.

STITCH GUIDE

Double Twisted Rib. Work through the back loop of every stitch on every row, knitting or purling as directed.

PATTERN NOTES

- The dress is worked flat in one piece. Sleeves are picked up at the shoulders and worked in the round.
- The colorwork is worked in intarsia. Use a separate ball (or length) of yarn for each section, and twist colors to prevent holes.
- Selvage stitches at each end are worked in plain St st and will be used to sew up seam at back of dress.

SKIRT

With Gray, cast on 506 (513, 520, 527, 534): 513 (527, 534, 541) sts. (For ease in counting, place a marker every 50 sts while casting on.)

Note: All sts except the first and last selvage stitch of each row are worked in Double Twisted Rib (work each stitch through the back loop).

Row 1 (WS): P1 (for selvage), work [p1b, k1b] Double Twisted Rib across to last st, p1.

Row 2 (RS): K1, work Double Twisted Rib (knit the knits, purl the purls, all through the back loop) across to last st, k1.

Work Row 1 again.

Begin intarsia:

(RS): With Gray, k1, work rib for 23 (24, 25, 26, 27): 24 (26, 27, 28) sts, join Green and work 49 sts, join Gray and work 23 (24, 25, 26, 27): 24 (26, 27, 28) sts, join Blue and work 49 sts, join Gray and work 23 (24, 25, 26, 27): 24 (26, 27, 28) sts, join Purple and work 49 sts, join Gray and work 23 (24, 25, 26, 27): 24 (26, 27, 28) sts, join Pink and work 49 sts, join Gray and work 23 (24, 25, 26, 27): 24 (26, 27, 28) sts, join Dark Pink and work 49 sts, join Gray and work 23 (24, 25, 26, 27): 24 (26, 27, 28) sts, join Orange and work 49 sts, join Gray and work 23 (24, 25, 26, 27): 24 (26, 27, 28) sts, join Yellow and work 49 sts, with Yellow k1 selvage st.

Next row (WS): P1 Yellow (for selvage), continue as established, working rib for all sts, grays over grays and colors over colors.

Note: Decreases are made at edges of 7 color bars only; Gray sts rem the same count throughout.

To work decreases on RS: K1 (selvage), *work across Gray as established, then with color work ssk, work to last 2 sts of color, k2tog; repeat from * across, k1 (selvage).

To work decreases on WS: P1 (selvage), *p2tog, work to last 2 sts of color, p2tog-tbl, work across Gray as established; repeat from * across, p1 (selvage).

Work decreases into edges of color bars (not Gray) every 5th (5th, 6th, 6th, 6th): 5th (6th, 6th, 7th) row 23 times (3 colored sts rem in each color bar section).

Work a further 5 (5, 6, 6, 6): 5 (6, 6, 7) rows as established, then decrease as follows:

If decrease row is on RS: K1 (selvage), *work Gray as established, then insert needle as if to knit through first two sts and slip off together to working needle, knit next st, pass both slipped sts over (1 color st rem); repeat from * to last st, k1 Yellow.

If decrease row is on WS: P1 Yellow, *slip next 2 sts through the back loop to working needle, purl next st, then pass the 2 slipped sts over (1 color st rem), work Gray as established; repeat from * across to last st, p1 (selvage) [170 (177, 184, 191, 198): 177 (191, 198, 205) sts rem]. Skirt should measure approx. 17 (17, 20, 20, 20): 17 (20, 20, 23) in. / 43 (43, 51, 51, 51): 43 (51, 51, 58.5) cm.

Intarsia is complete!

BODICE

Working with Gray only and keeping first and last st in stockinette for selvage, work in Double Twisted Rib for 3 (3, 3, 3, 5): 3 (5, 5, 5) rows. On any row, place markers as follows to mark sides: Work 42 (44, 46, 48, 49): 44 (48, 49, 51) sts, PM, work 86 (89, 92, 95, 100): 89 (96, 100, 103) sts for front, PM, work across rem 42 (44, 46, 48, 49): 44 (48, 49, 51) sts.

Increase row: Work one selvage st, work Double Twisted Rib to within one st of first marker, keeping rib pattern correct *knit and then purl (or purl and then knit) into the front and back of next st, SM, purl and then knit (or knit and then purl) into the front and back of next st*, work Double Twisted Rib to next marker, repeat from * to * once more, work in Double Twisted Rib to last st, work 1 selvage st.

Work increase row every 5th (5th, 6th, 6th, 6th): 5th (5th, 5th, 6th) row 6 times total to 48 (50, 52, 54, 55): 50 (54, 55, 57) sts for each back section and 98 (101, 104, 107, 112): 101 (107, 112, 115) sts for front.

Work even if necessary until bodice from end of color bars measures 3 (3½, 4, 4½, 5): 3½ (4, 4½, 5) in. / 7.5 (9, 10, 11.5, 12.5): 9 (10, 11.5, 12.5) cm, or desired length to armhole. End having completed a WS row.

Divide for front and backs:

(RS): Keeping selvage sts in stockinette at each end, work Double Twisted Rib to within 6 sts of first marker, bind off 12 sts in pattern (remove marker), work to within 6 sts of next marker, bind off 12 sts in pattern and complete row.

Place front sts and left back sts on a holder or waste yarn.

Right Back
ARMHOLE SHAPING

Next row (WS): P1, work in Double Twisted Rib as established to last 3 sts, p2tog, p1.

Next row (RS): K1, work across as established to last st, k1.

Repeat last 2 rows twice more [39 (41, 43, 45, 46): 41 (45, 46, 48) sts rem].

Work even as established until armhole from bind off measures 4½ (4½, 5, 5, 5½): 4½ (5, 5½, 5½) in. / 11.5 (11.5, 12.5, 12.5, 14): 11.5 (12.5, 14, 14) cm. End having completed a RS row.

NECK SHAPING

(WS): Work across 12 (13, 14, 15, 14): 12 (15, 14, 15) sts and place on a holder or waste yarn and continue across row.

Next row (RS): K1, work in Double Twisted Rib to last 3 sts, k2tog, k1.

Next row (WS): P1, work across to last st, p1.

Repeat last 2 rows twice more [24 (25, 26, 27, 29): 26 (27, 29, 30) sts rem].

Work one RS row without decreases.

Next row (WS): Work across 17 (18, 19, 20, 22): 19 (20, 22, 23) sts, w&t, work back on RS.

Next row (WS): Work across 10 (11, 12, 13, 15): 12 (13, 15, 16) sts, w&t, work back on RS.

Work one more row, picking up wraps across. Place sts on a holder or waste yarn.

Note: To pick up wrap on a knit st, insert needle into wrap first, then st on needle and knit the two together. To pick up a wrap on a purl st, pick up the wrap from behind and place it on the left needle, then purl the two sts together. Wraps will disappear into the work.

Left Back

Place 42 (44, 46, 48, 49): 44 (48, 49, 51) back sts on a needle.

Join new yarn on RS and begin with next row:

ARMHOLE SHAPING

Next row (RS): K1, work across in Double Twisted Rib as established to last 3 sts, k2tog, k1.

Next row (WS): P1, work across in Double Twisted Rib to last st, p1.

Repeat last 2 rows twice more [39 (41, 43, 45, 46): 41 (45, 46, 48) sts rem].

Work even as established until armhole from bind-off measures 4½ (4½, 5, 5, 5½): 4½ (5, 5½, 5½) in. / 11.5 (11.5, 12.5, 12.5, 14): 11.5 (12.5, 14, 14) cm. End having completed a WS row.

NECK SHAPING

(RS): Work across 12 (13, 14, 15, 14): 12 (15, 14, 15) sts and place on a holder or waste yarn and continue across row.

Next row (WS): P1, work in Double Twisted Rib to last 3 sts, p2tog-tbl, p1.

Next row (RS): K1, work across to last st, k1.

Repeat last 2 rows twice more [24 (25, 26, 27, 29): 26 (27, 29, 30) sts rem].

Work one WS row with no decreases.

SHOULDER SHAPING

Next row (RS): Work across 17 (18, 19, 20, 22): 19 (20, 22, 23) sts, w&t, work back on WS.

Next row (RS): Work across 10 (11, 12, 13, 15): 12 (13, 15, 16) sts, w&t, work back on WS.

Work one more row, picking up wraps across. Place sts on a holder or waste yarn.

Front

Place 86 (89, 86, 92, 95): 89 (95, 100, 103) front sts on needle. Join new yarn on RS.

ARMHOLE SHAPING

(RS): K1, ssk, work in Double Twisted Rib as established to last 3 sts, k2tog, k1.

(WS): P1, work in Double Twisted Rib to last st, p1.

Repeat last 2 rows twice more to 80 (83, 86, 89, 96): 83 (89, 94, 97) sts.

Work even as established until armholes measure 3 (3, 3½, 3½, 4): 3 (3½, 3½, 4) in. / 7.5 (7.5, 9, 9, 10): 7.5 (9, 9, 10) cm from bind off. End having completed a WS row.

NECK SHAPING

(RS): Work across 53 (55, 57, 59, 64): 54 (59, 62, 64) sts. Place last 26 (27, 28, 29, 32): 25 (29, 30, 31) sts *just worked* to a holder or waste yarn for center front neck and continue across row.

Next row (WS): P1, work in Double Twisted Rib to last 3 sts, p2tog-tbl, p1.

Next row (RS): K1, work in Double Twisted Rib to last st, k1.

Repeat last 2 rows twice more.

Work even on rem 24 (25, 26, 27, 29): 26 (27, 29, 30) sts until armhole measures 4½ (5, 5, 5½, 6): 5 (5½, 6, 6) in. / 11.5 (12.5, 12.5, 14, 15): 12.5 (14, 15, 15) cm, or same as for back. End having completed a WS row.

SHOULDER SHAPING

Next row (RS): Work across 17 (18, 19, 20, 22): 19 (20, 22, 23) sts, w&t, work back on WS.

Next row (RS): Work across 10 (11, 12, 13, 15): 12 (13, 15, 16) sts, w&t, work back on WS.

Work one more row across all sts, picking up wraps, and place on a holder or waste yarn.

Join new yarn at right front from the WS and work neck shaping as follows:

(WS): P1, p2tog, work in Double Twisted Rib to last st, p1.

(RS): K1, work in Double Twisted Rib to last st, k1.

Repeat last 2 rows twice more.

Work even on rem 24 (25, 26, 27, 29): 26 (27, 29, 30) sts until armhole measures 4½ (5, 5, 5½, 6): 5 (5½, 6, 6) in. / 11.5 (12.5, 12.5, 14, 15): 12.5 (14, 15, 15) cm. End having completed a RS row.

Next row (WS): Work across 17 (18, 19, 20, 22): 19 (20, 22, 23) sts, w&t, work back on RS.

Next row (WS): Work across 10 (11, 12, 13, 15): 12 (13, 15, 16) sts, w&t, work back on RS.

Work one more row across all sts, picking up wraps.

Use the three-needle bind-off (see page 117) to connect shoulders together from the WS.

Stitch back seam together.

SLEEVES (make two)

Begin at center of underarm and pick up and knit 86 (86, 92, 92, 100): 86 (92, 100, 100) sts. Place a marker for beginning of round and work as follows:

K1, work Double Twisted Rib to last st, k1.

Work 1 rnd as established.

Decrease round: K1, ssk, work in Double Twisted Rib to within 3 sts of marker, k2tog, k1.

Work a decrease rnd every 6th (7th, 7th, 8th, 8th): 6th (8th, 8th, 8th) rnd 15 (13, 14, 13, 15): 15 (13, 15, 15) times total to 56 (60, 64, 66, 70): 56 (66, 70, 70) sts.

Work even if necessary until sleeve from armhole measures 12 (13, 14, 15½, 16½): 13½ (15½, 16½, 17½) in. / 30.5 (33, 35.5, 39.5, 42): 34.5 (39.5, 42, 44.5) cm, or desired length of sleeve. Bind off loosely in pattern.

NECKBAND

Begin at right back shoulder and pick up and knit stitch
for stitch around neckline, working 2 sts together at
back seam. Adjust if necessary to make twisted rib
pattern correct. Place marker and work 1½ in. / 4 cm
(or desired length) in twisted rib. Bind off loosely in
pattern.

FINISHING

Weave in any loose ends, sew buttons over colored tri-
angles and on sleeves as shown in photos, if desired,
and steam lightly or block according to directions on
ball band.

red coat

This Seed stitch coat is fashioned with panels in front to mimic seam lines, with vertical pockets and I-cord finish around the entire coat. The decorative belt with buttons adds class to this comfortable cardigan coat.

SIZES
All girls' sizes 6 (7, 8, 9, 10) 12
Instructions are written for size 6; all other sizes follow. For ease in knitting, circle your size before beginning.

FINISHED MEASUREMENTS
Chest: 27 (28½, 30, 31½, 33) 34 in. / 68.5 (47, 76, 80, 84) 86.5 cm
Waist: 24 (25½, 27, 28½, 30) 31 in. / 61 (65, 68.5, 76) 78.5 cm
Total length: 24 (26, 27½, 29½, 31) 32 in. / 61 (66, 70, 75, 78.5) 81.5 cm

YARN
Lion Brand Heartland; 5 oz. / 142 g each approx. 251 yd. / 230 m; 94% acrylic, 6% rayon
- 8 (9, 9, 9, 10) 10 skeins #113 Redwood

MATERIALS
- Size US 6 / 4 mm 24 in. / 61 cm circular needle (*or size to obtain gauge*)
- Tapestry needle
- Waste yarn
- Pin-type markers
- Seven 1¼ in. / 3 cm buttons

GAUGE
22 sts and 36 rows to 4 in. / 10 cm in Seed st

STITCH GUIDE

Seedfb. Knit, then purl (or purl, then knit) into next stitch to keep seed pattern correct.

Seed2tog. Knit or purl 2 sts together, keeping the seed st pattern correct.

Seed Stitch (Seed st)
Row 1 (RS): [K1, p1] across.
Row 2 and all other rows: Knit the purls and purl the knits.

PATTERN NOTES

- This Seed stitch sweater coat has vertical pockets and an attached I-cord finish from cast-on or side edges (see page 117 for instructions).
- Although both sides of the Seed stitch fabric look the same, it's important to mark a "right side" to work proper shaping later.
- Every row begins with a slipped st (slipped purlwise with yarn in front) and ends with a knit st. This forms a neat chain to pick up easily for I-cord and a beautiful seam to whipstitch from the right side.
- See page 117 for instructions on how to work the attached I-cord.

BACK

Note: Back is worked in two pieces to form kick pleat, then joined and finished as one piece.

Left Back

Cast on 46 (49, 51, 54, 57) 60 sts.

(RS): With yarn in front, slip first st purlwise, then work in Seed st to last st, k1. Mark this row as the RS.

To work a decrease row on RS: Sl1, continue in Seed st to last 3 sts, seed2tog, k1.

To work a decrease row on WS: Sl1, seed2tog, continue in Seed st to last st, k1.

Work a decrease row every 9th row 6 (7, 7, 7, 7) 8 times total to 40 (42, 44, 47, 50) 52 sts.

Work one WS row and place all sts on a holder or waste yarn.

Right Back

Cast on 55 (58, 60, 63, 66) 69 sts.

(RS): With yarn in front, slip first st purlwise, then work in Seed st to last st, k1. Mark this row as the RS.

To work a decrease row on RS: Sl1, seed2tog, continue in Seed st to last st, k1.

To work a decrease row on WS: Sl1, continue in Seed st to last 3 sts, seed2tog, k1.

Work a decrease row every 9th row 6 (7, 7, 7, 7) 8 times total to 49 (51, 53, 56, 59) 61 sts.

On next WS row (this counts as Row 1, we're still decreasing) bind off first 9 sts, then continue across row.

Work across RS (Row 2), then place sts from left back onto needles and work across [80 (84, 88, 94, 100) 104 sts total].

Row 2 complete, backs joined; bound-off flap will be tucked under left back and stitched down on the inside.

To work a decrease row: Sl1, seed2tog, work Seed st to last 3 sts, seed2tog, k1.

Continue decreasing every 9th row 7 (7, 7, 8, 9) 9 times more to 66 (70, 74, 78, 82) 86 sts.

Work even if necessary until piece from cast-on edge measures approx. 13 (14½, 14½, 15½, 17) 17½ in. / 33 (37, 37, 39.5, 43) 44.5 cm, or desired length to waist. Hang a pin-type marker here for easy measuring.

Waist to Bust Shaping

To work an increase row: Sl1, seedfb, work in Seed st to last 2 sts, seedfb, k1.

Work an increase row every 4th (4th, 5th, 5th, 6th) 6th row 8 times total to 82 (86, 90, 94, 98) 102 sts.

Work even if necessary until piece from beginning of waist shaping measures 4 (4, 4½, 5, 5½) 5½ in. / 10 (10, 11.5, 12.5, 14) 14 cm. End having completed a WS row.

Armhole Shaping

Note: For ease in measuring depth of armhole, place a hanging marker somewhere in the middle of the row.

Beginning with a RS row, bind off 8 sts at the beginning of the next 2 rows [66 (70, 74, 78, 82) 86 sts rem].

Next row (RS): Sl1, seed2tog, work Seed st to last 3 sts, seed2tog, k1.

Next row: Sl1, knit to end.

Work last 2 rows 4 times more to 56 (60, 64, 68, 72) 76 sts.

When armhole measures 3½ (4, 4, 4½, 4½) 4½ in. / 9 (10, 10, 11.5, 11.5) 11.5 cm, work increases at armhole edge (seedfb, same as above) as follows for your size: Work an increase row *now*, and then every 6th (6th, 7th, 7th, 7th) 8th row 4 times more to 66 (70, 74, 78, 82) 86 sts.

Continue on these sts (if necessary) until total length of armhole measures 6½ (7, 7½, 8, 8) 8½ in. / 16.5 (18, 19, 20.5, 20.5) 21.5 cm. End having completed a WS row.

Back Neck Shaping

Note: Remember to slip the first st of every row.

(RS): Work across 48 (52, 55, 58, 60) 63 sts, place last 30 (34, 36, 38, 38) 40 sts *just worked* onto a holder or waste yarn and continue across last 18 (18, 19, 20, 22) 23 sts.

Row 1 (WS): Sl1, work Seed st to last 3 sts, seed2tog, k1.

Row 2 (RS): Sl1, seed2tog, work Seed st to last st, k1.

Repeat Row 1 [15 (15, 16, 17, 19) 20 sts rem].

Shoulder Shaping

Next row (RS): Sl1, work Seed st to last 3 (3, 3, 3, 4) 4 sts, w&t. Work back as established.

Next row (RS): Sl1, seed to last 6 (6, 6, 6, 8) 8 sts, w&t. Work back as established.

Next row (RS): Sl1, seed to last 9 (9, 9, 9, 12) 12 sts, w&t. Work back as established.

Next row (RS): Sl1, seed to last 12 (12, 12, 12, 16) 16 sts, w&t. Work back as established.

Work one more row and pick up wraps (place wrap on left needle and work it together with next st). Place live sts on a holder or waste yarn.

Other Side, Back Neck Shaping

Join new yarn at other edge from the WS and shape back neck as follows:

Row 1 (WS): Sl1, seed2tog, work Seed st to last st, k1.

Row 2 (RS): Sl1, work Seed st to last 3 sts, seed2tog, k1.

Work Row 1 again [15 (15, 16, 17, 19) 20 sts rem].

Next row (RS): Sl1, work Seed st to last st, k1.

Shoulder Shaping

Next row (RS): Sl1, work Seed st to last 3 (3, 3, 3, 4) 4 sts, w&t. Work back as established.

Next row (RS): Sl1, work Seed st to last 6 (6, 6, 6, 8) 8 sts, w&t. Work back as established.

Next row (RS): Sl1, work Seed st to last 9 (9, 9, 9, 12) 12 sts, w&t. Work back as established.

Next row (RS): Sl1, work Seed st to last 12 (12, 12, 12, 16) 16 sts, w&t. Work back as established.

Work one more row and pick up wraps. Place live sts on a holder or waste yarn.

FRONTS

Note: Each front is worked in two sections to form a vertical pocket opening and a decorative seam through the bust shaping. For accuracy in joining, pieces are worked simultaneously from armhole. Place pin-type markers wherever you can to denote areas of importance for ease in measuring.

Left Front, Section A

Cast on 24 (26, 28, 30, 30) 32 sts.

(RS): With yarn in front, slip first st purlwise, then work in Seed st to last st, knit last st. Mark this row as the RS.

Continue in Seed st (remember to slip first st and knit last st) with no decreases until piece measures 13 (14½, 14½, 15½, 17) 17½ in. / 33 (37, 37, 39.5, 43) 44.5 cm from beginning (or same length as back to waist). Mark as waist and continue with no shaping until total length measures 17 (18½, 19, 20½, 21½) 22½ in. / 43 (47, 48.5, 52, 54.5) 57 cm. Place sts on a holder or waste yarn. Do not cut yarn.

Left Front, Section B

Cast on 30 (32, 34, 36, 38) 40 sts.

(RS): With yarn in front, slip first st purlwise, then work in Seed st to last st, k1. Mark this row as the RS.

To work a decrease row on RS: Sl1, seed2tog, work Seed st to last st, k1.

To work a decrease row on WS: Sl1, work Seed st to last 3 sts, seed2tog, k1.

Work a decrease row every 9th row 13 (14, 14, 15, 17) 17 times total to 17 (18, 20, 21, 21) 23 sts.

Continue until piece measures 13 (14½, 14½, 15½, 17) 17½ in. / 33 (37, 37, 39.5, 43) 44.5 cm from beginning (or same length as back). End having completed a WS row. Mark for waist.

Waist to Bust Shaping

To work an increase row on RS: Sl1, seedfb, work Seed st to last st, k1.

To work an increase row on WS: Sl1, work Seed st to last 2 sts, seedfb, k1.

Work an increase row every 4th (4th, 5th, 5th, 6th) 6th row 8 times total to 25 (26, 28, 29, 29) 31 sts.

Work even if necessary until piece from beginning of waist shaping measures 4 (4, 4½, 5, 5½) 5½ in. / 10 (10, 11.5, 12.5, 14) 14 cm. End having completed a WS row.

Armhole Shaping

Note: For ease in measuring depth of armhole, place a hanging marker somewhere in the middle of the row.

(RS): Bind off 5 sts at the beginning of the next row (yes, less than for back): 20 (21, 23, 24, 24) 26 sts rem. At end of row, place all sts from Section A onto needle and work across.

Both pieces will now be worked separately, but at the same time, each with its own yarn. Section A will have *no shaping* while the armhole is shaped on the right side of Section B.

Next row (WS): Section A: Sl1, work Seed st to last st, k1. Section B: Sl1, work Seed st to last st, k1.

Next row (RS): Section B: Sl1, seed2tog, work to last st, k1. Section A: work across as established.

Work last 2 rows 4 times more to 15 (16, 18, 19, 19) 21 sts on section B. Section A will have original 24 (26, 28, 30, 30) 32 sts.

Work across one WS row on both sections.

Begin shaping on both sections as follows:

Note: Section B will now decrease by one st at the same time Section A increases.

Row 1 (RS): Section B: Sl1, work Seed st across to last 3 sts, seed2tog, k1. Section A: Sl1, seedfb, work to last st, k1.

Row 2 (WS): Work across both sections as established.

Repeat Rows 1 and 2 until one st rem on Section B. On next row, work it together with first st on Section A. Cut yarn from Section B.

Sections are now joined; adjust sts if necessary on next row to 39 (42, 46, 49, 49) 53 sts.

Piece should measure approx. 3½ (3½, 4, 4, 4) 4½ in. / 9 (9, 10, 10, 10) 11.5 cm from beginning of underarm shaping. Place a pin marker at front edge now to aid in measuring for depth of neck.

Increase row on RS: Sl1, seedfb, work Seed st to last st, k1.

Increase row on WS: Sl1, work Seed st to last 2 sts, seedfb, k1.

Work an increase row *now*, and then every 6th (6th, 7th, 7th, 7th) 8th row 3 times more to 43 (46, 50, 53, 53) 57 sts.

Continue on these sts (if necessary) until total length of armhole measures 5 (5½, 6, 6½, 6½) 7 in. / 12.5 (14, 15, 16.5, 16.5) 18 cm, or 1½ in. / 4 cm less than back). End having completed a RS row.

Front Neck Shaping

(WS): Bind off 12 (13, 13, 14, 14) 14 sts. Work across next 13 (15, 18, 19, 17) 20 sts [14 (16, 19, 20, 18) 21 sts on needle] and place sts *just worked* on a holder or waste yarn; work across rem 18 (18, 19, 20, 22) 23 sts.

Row 1 (RS): Sl1, work Seed st to last 3 sts, seed2tog, k1.

Row 2 (WS): Sl1, work Seed st to last st, k1.

Work Rows 1 and 2 twice more, then work Row 1 [15 (15, 16, 17, 19) 20 sts rem].

Work even (if necessary) until armhole measures same as for back. End having completed a RS row.

Shoulder Shaping

Next row (WS): Sl1, work Seed st to last 3 (3, 3, 3, 4) 4 sts, w&t. Work back as established.

Next row (WS): Sl1, work Seed st to last 6 (6, 6, 6, 8) 8 sts, w&t. Work back as established.

Next row (WS): Sl1, work Seed st to last 9 (9, 9, 9, 12) 12 sts, w&t. Work back as established.

Next row (WS): Sl1, work Seed st to last 12 (12, 12, 12, 16) 16 sts, w&t. Work back as established.

Work one more row and pick up wraps (place wrap on left needle and work it together with next st). Place live sts on a holder or waste yarn.

Right Front, Section A (with Buttonholes)

Note: For placement of buttonholes, lay out completed left front on a table. Hook a pin-type marker around any chain at the front edge where the waist shaping begins. Place another marker ½ in. / 1.5 cm from top at neck. From there, you can count the chains and divide equally for the two buttons in between, and count chains for the buttonhole below the waist shaping (5 buttons total). While knitting section A, the marked buttonhole rows on the left front will denote placement of buttonhole rows. Make note of the number of rows between buttonholes, or the measurement in inches.

Cast on 24 (26, 28, 30, 30) 32 sts.

(RS): With yarn in front, slip first st purlwise, then work in Seed st to last st, k1. Mark this row as the RS.

Continue in Seed St (remember to slip first st and knit last st) with no decreases until piece measures same as left front to designated first buttonhole. End having completed a WS row.

Buttonhole row 1 (RS): Sl1, work 2 sts in Seed st, bind off 3 sts, knit to end.

Buttonhole row 2 (WS): Sl1, work to bound off sts, turn work and cast-on 3 sts with the knitted cast on, turn back, work 2 sts in Seed st, k1.

Continue with buttonholes at the intervals calculated until total length measures 17 (18½, 19, 20½, 21½) 22½ in. / 43 (47, 48.5, 52, 54.5) 57 cm from beginning. End having completed a RS row.

Place sts on a holder or waste yarn. Do not cut yarn. Note where you are in buttonhole placement as they will continue when front sections are joined.

Right Front, Section B

Cast on 30 (32, 34, 36, 38) 40 sts.

(RS): With yarn in front, slip first st purlwise, then work in Seed st to last st, k1. Mark this row as the RS.

To work a decrease row on RS: Sl1, work in Seed st to last 3 sts, seed2tog, k1.

To work a decrease row on WS: Sl1, seed2tog, work in
Seed st to last st, k1.

Work a decrease row every 9th row 13 (14, 14, 15, 17) 17
times total to 17 (18, 20, 21, 21) 23 sts.

When piece measures 13 (14½, 14½, 15½, 17) 17½ in. /
33 (37, 37, 39.5, 43) 44.5 cm from beginning (or same
length as back), end having completed a WS row,
and place a marker for waist.

Waist to Bust Shaping

To work an increase row on RS: Sl1, work Seed st to last
2 sts; seedfb, k1.

To work an increase row on WS: Sl1, seedfb, work Seed
st to last st, k1.

Work an increase row every 4th (4th, 5th, 5th, 6th) 6th
row 8 times total to 25 (26, 28, 29, 29) 31 sts.

Work even (if necessary) until piece from beginning
of waist shaping measures 4 (4, 4½, 5, 5½) 5½ in. /
10 (10, 11.5, 12.5, 14) 14 cm. End having completed a
RS row.

Armhole Shaping

Note: For ease in measuring depth of armhole, place a
hanging marker somewhere in the middle of the row.

(WS): Bind off 5 sts at the beginning of the next row:
20 (21, 23, 24, 24) 26 sts rem. At end of row, place all
sts from Section A onto needle and work across.

Both pieces will now be worked separately, but at the
same time, each with its own yarn. Section A will
have no shaping (remember to continue with buttonholes), while the armhole is shaped on the wrong
side of Section B,

Next row (RS): Section A: Sl1, work Seed st to last st, k1.
Section B: Sl1, work Seed st to last st, k1.

Next row (WS): Section B: Sl1, seed2tog, work Seed st
to last st, k1. Section A: Work across as established.

Work last 2 rows 4 times more to 15 (16, 18, 19, 19) 21
sts on Section B. Section A will have original 24 (26,
28, 30, 30) 32 sts.

Work across one RS row on both sections.

Note: Continue where you left off with buttonhole
placement on Section A.

Begin shaping on both sections as follows:

Note: Section B will now decrease by one st at the same
time Section A increases.

Row 1 (WS): Section B: Sl1, work Seed st across to last 3
sts, seed2tog, k1. Section A: Sl1, seedfb, work Seed st
to last st, k1.

Row 2 (RS): Work across both sections as established.

Repeat Rows 1 and 2 until one st rem on Section B. On
next row, work it together with first st on Section A.
Cut yarn from Section B.

Sections are now joined; adjust sts, if necessary, on next
row to 39 (42, 46, 49, 49) 53 sts.

Piece should measure approx. 3½ (3½, 4, 4, 4) 4½ in. /
9 (9, 10, 10, 10) 11.5 cm from beginning of underarm
shaping. Place a pin marker at front edge now to aid
in measuring for depth of neck.

Increase row on RS: Sl1, work Seed st to last 2 sts,
seedfb, k1.

Increase row on WS: Sl1, seedfb, work Seed st to last
st, k1.

Work an increase row now, and then every 6th (6th, 7th,
7th, 7th) 8th row 3 times more to 43 (46, 50, 53, 53)
57 sts.

Continue on these sts, if necessary, until total length of
armhole measures 5 (5½, 6, 6½, 6½) 7 in. / 12.5 (14,
15, 16.5, 16.5) 18 cm, or 1½ in. / 4 cm less than back.
End having completed a WS row.

Front Neck Shaping

(RS): Bind off 12 (13, 13, 14, 14) 14 sts. Work across next
13 (15, 18, 19, 17) 20 sts [14 (16, 19, 20, 18) 21 sts
on needle] and place sts just worked on a holder or
waste yarn, work across rem 18 (18, 19, 20, 22) 23 sts.

Row 1 (WS): Sl1, work Seed st to last 3 sts, seed2tog, k1.

Row 2 (RS): Sl1, work Seed st to last st, k1.

Work Rows 1 and 2 twice more, then work Row 1: 15 (15,
16, 17, 19) 20 sts rem.

Work even if necessary until armhole measures same as
for back. End having completed a WS row.

Shoulder Shaping

Next row (RS): Sl1, work Seed st to last 3 (3, 3, 3, 4) 4
sts, w&t. Work back as established.

Next row (RS): Sl1, work Seed st to last 6 (6, 6, 6, 8) 8
sts, w&t. Work back as established.

Next row (RS): Sl1, work Seed st to last 9 (9, 9, 9, 12) 12
sts, w&t. Work back as established.

Next row (RS): Sl1, work Seed st to last 12 (12, 12, 12, 16)
16 sts, w&t. Work back as established.

COLLAR

Place all live sts from front and back neck on a needle. From RS, join new yarn at right front and work in pattern around, picking up stitch for stitch on edges of neck shaping. Shoot for somewhere around 82 (84, 86, 88, 90) 94 sts for your size.

Row 1: Sl1, work Seed st to last st, k1.

Repeat Row 1 until collar measures 3½ (3½, 3½, 4, 4) 4 in. / 9 (9, 9, 10, 10) 10 cm, or desired width. Bind off in pattern.

SLEEVES (make two)

At underarm, from RS, place a marker after first and before last 5 sts; join yarn and pick up and knit 70 (76, 80, 86, 86) 90 sts around armhole edge between markers.

Next row (WS): Sl1, work Seed st to last st, slip last st to right needle, then pick up bound-off st from underarm and place on left needle. Put slipped st back to left needle and knit it together with bound-off st.

Repeat last row until all bound-off sts are worked into sleeve [stitch count doesn't change: 70 (76, 80, 86, 86) 90 sts rem].

Work 9 (7, 7, 6, 6) 6 rows.

Decrease row: Sl1, seed2tog, work Seed st to last 3 sts, seed2tog, k1.

Work a decrease row every 10th (8th, 8th, 7th, 7th) 7th row 12 (15, 16, 19, 18) 20 times total [46 (46, 48, 48, 50) 50 sts rem].

Work even if necessary until sleeve from underarm measures 14½ (15, 15½, 16, 16½) 17 in. / 37 (38, 39.5, 40.5, 42) 43 cm, or desired length.

Bind off using the I-cord bind-off (see page 117).

Work one more row and pick up wraps (place wrap on left needle and work it together with next st).

Use the three-needle bind-off (see page 117) to connect shoulders together from the RS (for a decorative seam).

Seam front panels together as follows:

Beginning at bottom edge, whipstitch chains until seam measures 6 (7, 7, 7, 8) 8½ in. / 15 (18, 18, 18, 20.5) 21.5 cm. Secure and cut yarn (leave a tail for weaving). Leave an opening of 5 (5½, 5½, 6, 6½) 6½ in. / 12.5 (14, 14, 15, 16.5) 16.5 cm for pocket, join new yarn, and seam to armhole edge. Fronts are now complete.

POCKET LINERS

Right Front: From the RS, at edge closest to side of coat, pick up stitch for stitch through back loop only of chains along pocket opening. Turn and work back on WS, casting on 10 sts at beginning of next row. Work back and forth in Seed st until pocket liner measures just short of buttonhole. Bind off in pattern.

Work left front pocket the same. Turn pocket liners to inside of coat and stitch into place.

BELT

Cast on 10 sts (or as many as desired for width of belt).
Row 1: Sl1, work Seed st to last st, k1.
Repeat Row 1 until belt measures the length from front
    panel at seam around the back to other side front
    panel seam.
Finish with I-cord bind-off. At end of row, turn work
    clockwise and continue with attached I-cord around
    the finished edges.

FINISHING

Sew side and underarm seams from the RS using a
    whipstitch into each chained edge st.
Stitch belt around back to seam between Sections A
    and B. Sew on two decorative buttons.
Sew five buttons opposite buttonholes.
Weave in all ends.
From the RS, beginning at bottom side edge, work
    I-cord edging around entire coat. Graft or join
    attached I-cord ends together and weave in ends.

plaid skirt

Knit entirely in the round, this Plaid Skirt gives the knitter who is comfortable with stranded colorwork a fun piece that any girl would love to wear. The beginner knitter could omit all of the colorwork and knit the whole piece in a solid or variegated color. The twisted rib band eliminates the need for elastic, but directions are given for a casing if you prefer to add it.

SIZES
Girls 6 (7, 8, 10, 12): Young Juniors 5/6 (7/8, 9/10, 11/12)
Instructions are written for size 6; all other sizes follow. Girls and Young Juniors sizes are separated with a colon. For ease in knitting, circle your size before beginning.

FINISHED MEASUREMENTS
Waist: 21 (22½, 23½, 24½, 25½): 22½ (24½, 25½, 26½) in. / 53.5 (57, 59.5, 62, 65): 57 (62, 65, 67.5) cm
Skirt length from waist: 14 (14½, 15, 15, 15½): 14½ (15, 15½, 15½) in. / 35.5 (37, 38, 38, 39.5) cm: 37 (38, 39.5, 39.5) cm

YARN
Cascade Yarns Heritage 150; 5.3 oz. / 150 g each approx. 492 yd. / 450 m; 75% merino wool, 25% nylon
  • 1 skein #5672 Real Black (A)
  • 1 skein #5607 Red (B)
Note: You will use nearly the whole skein of black for this pattern as written up to size young junior 7/8. To make a longer skirt or a larger size, you may either make the waistband in red or purchase an additional skein of black.

MATERIALS
  • Size US 3 / 3.25 mm 24 in. / 61 cm or longer circular needle (*or size to obtain gauge*)
  • Tapestry needle
  • Waste yarn
  • Elastic for waistband, no more than 1 in. / 2.5 cm wide (optional)
  • Ring-type markers, 18 total (17 of one color and 1 for beg of round)

GAUGE
26 sts and 32 rows to 4 in. / 10 cm in St st

PATTERN NOTES

- The skirt is knit in the round from the bottom up using Fair Isle method, twisting colors every few sts to avoid long floats.
- See page 117 for instructions on how to work an I-cord cast-on.

SKIRT

Helpful hint: Place a marker every 18 sts as you cast on.

With A (Black), cast on using the I-cord cast-on to end up with 288 (288, 288, 324, 324): 288 (324, 324, 324) sts. Place a different color marker and join in the round, being careful not to twist sts.

Begin pattern:

*Work 18 sts of Rnd 1 Chart A, PM (if not already done), 18 sts Rnd 1 Chart B, PM; repeat from * 7 (7, 7, 8, 8): 7 (8, 8, 8) times more.

Continue as established, working decreases on Rnd 13 of Chart B as follows: *Work Chart A, SM, ssk, work to within 2 sts of next marker, k2tog, SM; repeat from * around [16 (16, 16, 18, 18): 16 (18, 18, 18) sts decreased].

Work decrease rnd every 13th rnd until 2 sts rem for Chart B (chart shows only 100 rows; keep going until 2 sts rem on Chart B).

On the next few rnds, decrease stitch count to 140 (146, 154, 160, 168): 146 (160, 168, 174) sts.

Continue with no further decreases until total length of skirt is 12½ (13, 13½, 13½, 14): 13 (13½, 14, 14) in. / 32 (33, 34.5, 34.5, 35.5): 33 (34.5, 35.5, 35.5) cm, or desired length. *Note:* If longer skirt is desired, the waistband might have to be knitted entirely in red, or you may need to purchase another skein of black, as the one skein of black will run out.

WAISTBAND

Change to Black and knit one round.

Next rnd: *K1b, p1b; repeat from * around.

Repeat this rnd until waistband casing measures 3 in. / 7.5 cm. *Note:* If you run out of black, knit one rnd in red (to make a straight line), then resume [k1b, p1b] pattern. This will be on the inside and won't show.

Bind off loosely in pattern.

Turn casing and stitch down to inside, leaving an opening to insert elastic, if desired.

FINISHING

Optional: Cut elastic 1 in. / 2.5 cm shorter than waist
measurement and thread through waistband casing.
Sew elastic ends together, then stitch down casing
opening.

Weave in any ends and steam lightly or block according to directions on ball band.

CHART A

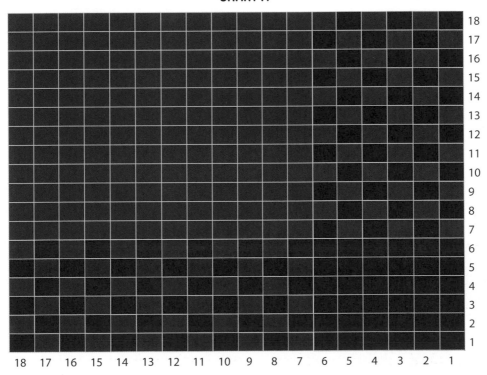

Color A
Color B

CHART B

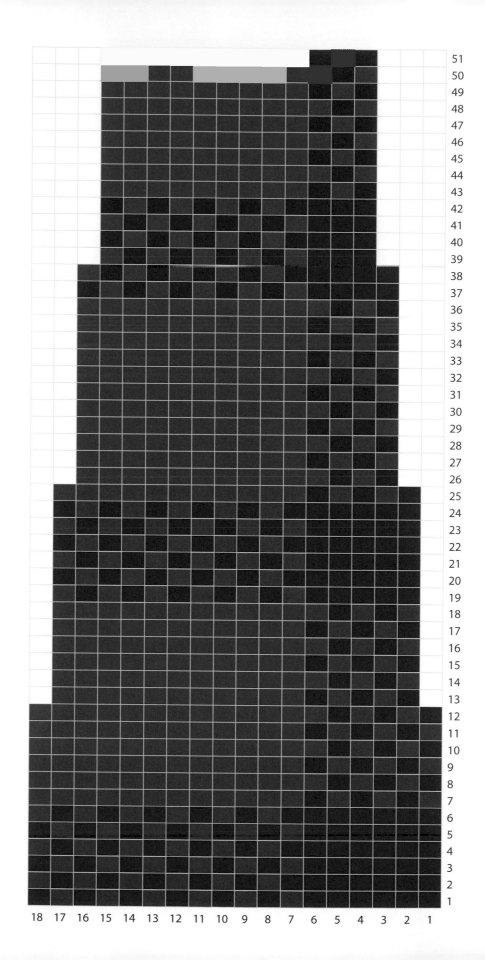

Color A
Color B

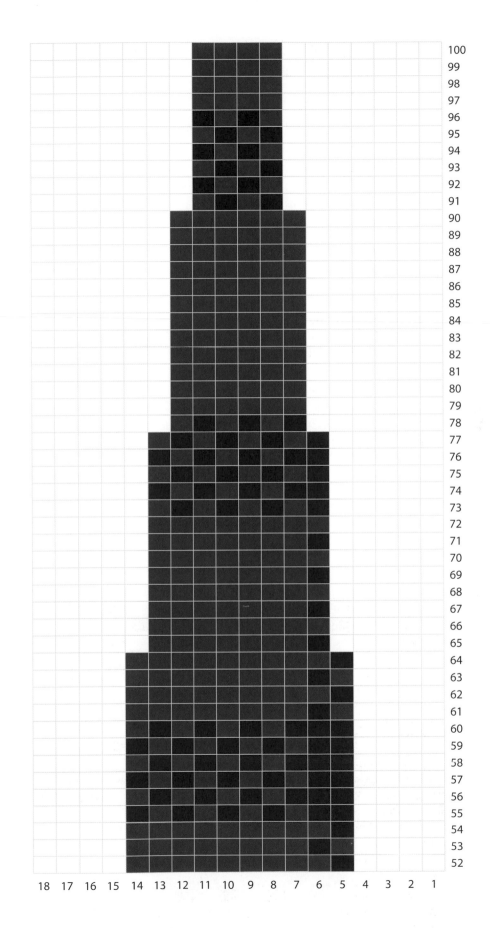

Color A
Color B

100
99
98
97
96
95
94
93
92
91
90
89
88
87
86
85
84
83
82
81
80
79
78
77
76
75
74
73
72
71
70
69
68
67
66
65
64
63
62
61
60
59
58
57
56
55
54
53
52

18 17 16 15 14 13 12 11 10 9 8 7 6 5 4 3 2 1

black top

Designed in Garter stitch with no shaping for the brand-new knitter, this versatile top is made from two squares sewn together. If the attached I-cord and I-cord bind-off seem intimidating, you can use a standard cast-on and bind-off, and you will still have a great result.

SIZES

Girls 6 (7, 8, 10) 12: Young Juniors 5/6 (7/8, 9/10, 11/12)
Instructions are written for size 6; all other sizes follow. Girls and Young Juniors sizes are separated with a colon. For ease in knitting, circle your size before beginning.

FINISHED MEASUREMENTS

Chest measurement: 28 (29, 30, 31) 32: 33 (34, 36, 38) in. / 71 (73.5, 76, 78.5) 81: 84 (86.5, 91.5, 96.5) cm
Length: 12½ (13½, 14½, 15½) 16: 13½ (14½, 15½, 16½) in. / 32 (34.5, 37, 39.5) 40.5: 34.5 (37, 39.5, 42) cm

YARN

Cascade Yarns Heritage 150; 5.3 oz. / 150 g each approx. 492 yd. / 450 m; 75% merino wool, 25% nylon
- 2 skeins (all sizes) #5672 Real Black

MATERIALS

- Size US 3 / 3.25 mm needles (or size to obtain gauge)
- Tapestry needle

GAUGE

26 sts and 52 rows to 4 in. / 10 cm in Garter stitch

PATTERN NOTES

- This easy top has no shaping. It has drop shoulders and an attached I-cord finish.
- See page 117 for instructions on how to work the I-cord cast-on and bind-off, and the three-needle bind-off.

FRONT

Note: On every row, slip the first st purlwise with yarn in front, then put yarn back behind needle and continue across.

Cast on 91 (95, 98, 101) 104: 107 (110, 117, 123) sts.

Work in Garter stitch (knit all sts) with slip-stitch edge for 7½ (8, 8½, 8½) 9: 8 (8½, 8½, 9) in. / 19 (20.5, 21.5, 21.5) 23: 20.5 (21.5, 21.5, 23) cm. Place a marker at beginning and end of row for armhole placement.

Continue until total length measures 12½ (13½, 14½, 15½) 16: 13½ (14½, 15½, 16½) in. / 32 (34.5, 37, 39.5) 40.5: 34.5 (37, 39.5, 42) cm. Place 17 (19, 20, 19) 20: 25 (26, 27, 30) sts for each shoulder on a holder or waste yarn; place center 57 (57, 58, 63) 64: 57 (58, 63, 63) sts on waste yarn for neck and rem sts on a holder or waste yarn for other shoulder.

BACK

Work same as for front.

FINISHING

From the RS (binding off on the WS in the usual manner leaves a divot in garter st seams), use the three-needle bind-off to connect the shoulder sts together.

Begin at center back (or desired placement of I-cord seam) and place all live sts from front and back neck on needle and work I-cord bind-off from live stitches (page 117) around or simply bind off if you don't want to attempt the I-cord.

From the RS, whipstitch side seams to markers, leaving 5 (5½, 6, 7) / : 5½ (6, 7, 7½) in. / 12.5 (14, 15, 18) 18: 14 (15, 18, 19) cm unseamed for armhole.

Work attached I-cord from side edges (page 117) around each armhole opening and bottom edge.

Weave in any ends and steam lightly or block according to directions on ball band.

sparkle vest

Made of two easy Garter stitch pieces sewn together, this vest is suitable for the brand-new knitter. This vest can be made for adults, babies, and all sizes in between. Pick a yarn and a needle size, determine a gauge, make two measurements, and you're ready to go. The vest can be worn upside down or right side up. Working with a strand of plain yarn held with a strand of metallic yarn adds the sparkle, but any yarn can be used to make this versatile and fun vest.

SIZES
Sample directions written for child's small (medium, large), ages approx. 6 (9, 12)
Sizes are adjustable to fit anyone with any yarn at any gauge.

FINISHED MEASUREMENTS
"Scarf" piece: approx. 48 (53, 58) in. / 122 (134.5, 147.5) cm long
To customize, measure length as if you were wearing a scarf: begin where you want vest to hang at front, then around neck and down other front. This will be the length of your "scarf" piece.
Back: approx. 11 (12, 13) in. / 28 (30.5, 33) cm wide
To customize, measure across back from shoulder to shoulder.

YARN
Ella Rae Cozy Soft; 3.5 oz. / 100 g each approx. 213 yd. / 195 m; 25% superwash wool, 75% acrylic
• 3 skeins Navy
Premier Yarns Spangle; 1.7 oz. / 50 g each approx. 164 yd. / 150 m; 76% nylon, 25% metallic
• 4 skeins #208 Sparkling Water

MATERIALS
• Size US 10½ / 6.5 mm needles (*or any needles suitable for the yarn you choose*)
• Tapestry needle
• Pins

GAUGE

14 sts to 4 in. / 10 cm in Garter stitch with 2 strands
   held together

*Gauge is not critical for this project, but if you use a
   different yarn and needles a gauge swatch will be
   helpful for determining the number of stitches to cast
   on and pick up for the desired measurements.*

VEST

With 2 strands held together, cast on 36 (42, 48) sts
   (or number of stitches for desired width of "scarf"
   piece).

Row 1: Slip first st with yarn in front as if to purl, then
   put yarn to back and knit across row.

Repeat Row 1 until scarf measures 48 (53, 58) in. / 122
   (134.5, 147.5) cm or desired length.

Bind off.

Fold scarf in half to find the center and mark with a pin.

Using this as the halfway point, measure 5 (5½, 6) in. /
   12.5 (14, 15) cm (or half of desired width of back) on
   either side of center and mark this distance.

Pick up and knit 36 (42, 48) sts between markers (or
number needed) for the back piece.

Knit until piece measures 10 in. / 25.5 cm, or length to
match "scarf." To determine the total length of the
back, place vest on a hanger with shawl collar folded
over. Line up the back to the front and measure down
5 in. / 12.5 cm or desired depth from the shoulders
on both sides for armholes and pin the front and
back together to mark this point. Now you can easily
see how much more length you need to add to the
back to measure the same as the front.

Leave underarm markers where placed and finish knitting the back, if more length is needed. Bind off.

FINISHING

Sew side seams to underarm markers and weave in any
loose ends.

classic coat

Worked entirely in Garter stitch, this coat is easier than it looks. It's a classic look for any girl to wear with her favorite jeans, or dress it up for a special occasion.

SIZES
All Girls sizes 6 (7, 8, 9, 10) 12
Instructions are written for size 6; all other sizes follow.

FINISHED MEASUREMENTS
Chest: 29 (30, 32, 34, 36) 38 in. / 73.5 (76, 81.5, 86.5, 91.5) 96.5 cm

Total length: 24 (26, 27½, 29½, 31) 32 in. / 61 (66, 70, 75, 78.5) 81.5 cm

YARN
Berroco Ultra Alpaca; 3.5 oz. / 100 g each approx. 215 yd. / 198 m; 50% alpaca, 50% wool
- 8 (9, 9, 10, 10) 10 skeins #6289 Charcoal Mix

MATERIALS
- Size US 4 / 3.5 mm 24 in. / 61 cm circular needle (*or size to obtain gauge*)
- Tapestry needle
- Waste yarn
- Ring-type markers
- Twelve 1 in. / 2.5 cm buttons
- Pin-type markers

GAUGE
20 sts and 44 rows to 4 in. / 10 cm in Garter stitch

PATTERN NOTES
- This is a double-breasted sweater coat with attached I-cord (see page 117 for instructions).
- Although both sides look the same, it's important to mark a "right side" to work proper shaping later.
- Every row begins with a slipped st (slipped purlwise with yarn in front) and ends with a knit st. This forms a neat chain to pick up sts for I-cord from front edges.

BACK

Cast on 92 (98, 102, 108, 114) 120 sts.

(RS): With yarn in front, slip first st purlwise, then put yarn to back (between the two needles) and knit across. Slipping the first st of every row makes a neat chain along the front edge that you will use later. Mark this row as the RS.

To work a decrease row: Sl1, ssk, knit to last 3 sts, k2tog, k1.

Work a decrease row every 10th (11th, 12th, 12th, 12th) 13th row 15 (15, 15, 16, 16) 15 times total to 62 (68, 72, 76, 82) 90 sts.

Work even if necessary until piece from cast on measures approx. 13 (14½, 14½, 15½, 17) 17½ in. / 33 (37, 37, 39.5, 43) 44.5 cm (or desired length to waist).

Waist to Bust Shaping

To work an increase row: Sl1, kfb, work to last 2 sts, kfb, k1.

Work an increase row every 8th (8th, 9th, 11th, 11th) 11th row 4 times total to 70 (76, 80, 84, 90) 98 sts. End having completed a WS row.

Armhole Shaping

Note: For ease in measuring depth of armhole, place a hanging marker somewhere in the middle of the first row.

(RS): Bind off 5 sts at the beginning of the next 2 rows [60 (66, 70, 74, 80) 88 sts rem].

Next row (RS): Sl1, ssk, knit to last 3 sts, k2tog, k1.

Next row: Sl1, knit to end.

Work last 2 rows 4 times more to 50 (56, 60, 64, 70) 78 sts.

When armhole measures 3½ (4, 4, 4½, 4½) 4½ in. / 9 (10, 10, 11.5, 11.5) 11.5 cm, work increases (kfb, same as above) as follows for your size:

Work an increase row now, and then every 9th (8th, 8th, 8th, 8th) 8th row 4 times more to 60 (66, 70, 74, 80) 88 sts.

Continue on these sts (if necessary) until total length of armhole measures 6½ (7, 7½, 8, 8) 8½ in. / 16.5 (18, 19, 20.5, 20.5) 21.5 cm. End having completed a WS row.

Back Neck Shaping

Note: Remember to slip the first st of every row.

(RS): Work across 44 (49, 52, 55, 59) 64 sts, place last 28 (32, 34, 36, 38) 40 sts *just worked* onto a holder or waste yarn and continue across last 16 (17, 18, 19, 21) 24 sts.

Row 1 (WS): Sl1, knit to last 3 sts, k2tog, k1.

Row 2 (RS): Sl1, ssk, knit to end.

Repeat Row 1 [13 (14, 15, 16, 18) 21 sts rem].

Shoulder Shaping

Next row (RS): Sl1, knit to last 2 (2, 2, 2, 3) 3 sts, w&t. Work back.

Next row (RS): Sl1, knit to last 4 (4, 4, 4, 6) 6 sts, w&t. Work back.

Next row (RS): Sl1, knit to last 6 (6, 6, 6, 9) 9 sts, w&t. Work back.

Next row (RS): Sl1, knit to last 8 (8, 8, 8, 12) 12 sts, w&t. Work back.

Next row (RS): Sl1, knit to last 10 (10, 10, 10, 15) 15 sts, w&t. Work back.

Next row (RS): Sl1, knit to last 12 (12, 12, 12, 18) 18 sts, w&t. Work back.

Work one more row and pick up wraps (place wrap on left needle and knit it together with next st). Place live sts on a holder or waste yarn.

Other Side, Back Neck Shaping

Join new yarn at other edge from the WS and shape
   back neck as follows:

Row 1 (WS): Sl1, ssk, knit to end.

Row 2 (RS): Sl1, knit to last 3 sts, k2tog, k1.

Work Row 1 again [13 (14, 15, 16, 18) 21 sts rem].

Next row (RS): Sl1, knit to end.

Shoulder Shaping

Next row (WS): Sl1, knit to last 2 (2, 2, 2, 3) 3 sts, w&t.
   Work back.

Next row (WS): Sl1, knit to last 4 (4, 4, 4, 6) 6 sts, w&t.
   Work back.

Next row (WS): Sl1, knit to last 6 (6, 6, 6, 9) 9 sts, w&t.
   Work back.

Next row (WS): Sl1, knit to last 8 (8, 8, 8, 12) 12 sts, w&t.
   Work back.

Next row (WS): Sl1, knit to last 10 (10, 10, 10, 15) 15 sts,
   w&t. Work back.

Next row (WS): Sl1, knit to last 12 (12, 12, 12, 18) 18 sts,
   w&t. Work back.

Work one more row and pick up wraps. Place live sts on
   a holder or waste yarn.

POCKET LINERS (make two)

Cast on 20 (20, 23, 25, 25) 28 sts. Work in Garter st (no
   need to slip first st) until liner measures 4 (4, 4½, 5,
   5) 5½ in. / 10 (10, 11.5, 13, 13) 13 cm. Place sts on a
   holder or waste yarn.

Continue with decreases until piece measures approx. 13 (14½, 14½, 15½, 17) 17½ in. / 33 (37, 37, 39.5, 43) 44.5 cm from beginning (or same length as back).

Waist to Bust Shaping

To work an increase row on RS: Sl1, kfb, knit to end.
To work an increase row on WS: Sl1, knit to last 2 sts, kfb, k1.
Work an increase row every 8th (8th, 9th, 11th, 11th) 11th row 4 times total to 47 (51, 53, 54, 58) 61 sts. End having completed a WS row.

Armhole Shaping

Note: For ease in measuring depth of armhole, place a hanging marker somewhere in the middle of the first row.
(RS): Bind off 5 sts at the beginning of row, knit to end [42 (46, 48, 49, 53) 56 sts rem].
Next row (WS): Sl1, knit to last 3 sts, k2tog, k1.
Next row (RS): Sl1, knit to end.
Work last 2 rows 4 times more to 37 (41, 43, 44, 48) 51 sts.
When armhole measures 3½ (4, 4, 4½, 4½) 4½ in. / 9 (10, 10, 11.5, 11.5) 11.5 cm, end having completed a WS row.
Increase row (RS): Sl1, kfb, knit to end.
Work an increase row every 8th row 4 times more to 42 (46, 48, 49, 53) 56 sts.
Continue on these sts (if necessary) until total length of armhole measures 6 (6½, 7, 7½, 7½) 8 in. / 15 (16.5, 18, 19, 19) 20.5 cm. End having completed a RS row.

Front Neck Shaping

(WS): Bind off 13 (13, 14, 14, 15) 15 sts, knit next 12 (15, 15, 15, 16) 16 sts [13 (16, 16, 16, 17) 17 sts on needle] and place on a holder or waste yarn, and knit across rem 16 (17, 18, 19, 21) 24 sts.
Row 1 (RS): Sl1, knit to last 3 sts, k2tog, k1.
Row 2 (WS): Sl1, knit across.
Work Rows 1 and 2 twice more, then work Row 1.

Shoulder Shaping

Next row (WS): Sl1, knit to last 2 (2, 2, 2, 3) 3 sts, w&t. Work back.
Next row (WS): Sl1, knit to last 4 (4, 4, 4, 6) 6 sts, w&t. Work back.

LEFT FRONT

Cast on 58 (62, 64, 66, 70) 72 sts.
Sl1, knit across. Mark as RS.
To work a decrease row on RS: Sl1, ssk, knit to end.
To work a decrease row on WS: Sl1, knit to last 3 sts, k2tog, k1.
Work a decrease row every 10th (11th, 12th, 12th, 12th) 13th row 15 (15, 15, 16, 16) 15 times total to 43 (47, 49, 50, 54) 57 sts. **At the same time,** when work measures 8 (10½, 11, 12, 13½) 14 in. / 20.5 (26.5, 28, 30.5, 34.5) 35.5 cm, ending having completed a WS row, work pocket opening as follows:
(RS): Work across 10 sts, bind off 20 (20, 23, 25, 25) 28 sts, continue across row.
Next row: Work to bound-off sts, slip sts from pocket liner to left needle, knit them, and continue across row.

Next row (WS): Sl1, knit to last 6 (6, 6, 6, 9) 9 sts, w&t. Work back.

Next row (WS): Sl1, knit to last 8 (8, 8, 8, 12) 12 sts, w&t. Work back.

Next row (WS): Sl1, knit to last 10 (10, 10, 10, 15) 15 sts, w&t. Work back.

Next row (WS): Sl1, knit to last 12 (12, 12, 12, 18) 18 sts, w&t. Work back.

Work one more row and pick up wraps (place on left needle and knit together with next st). Place live sts on a holder or waste yarn.

RIGHT FRONT

Cast on 58 (62, 64, 66, 70) 72 sts.

Sl1, knit across. Mark as RS.

To work a decrease row on RS: Sl1, knit to last 3 sts, k2tog, k1.

To work a decrease row on WS: Sl1, ssk, knit to end.

Work a decrease row every 10th (11th, 12th, 12th, 12th) 13th row 15 (15, 15, 16, 16) 15 times total to 43 (47, 49, 50, 54) 57 sts. **At the same time**, when work measures 8 (10½, 11, 12, 13½) 14 in. / 20.5 (26.5, 28, 30.5, 34.5) 35.5 cm, ending having completed a WS row, work pocket opening as follows:

(RS): Work across to last 30 (30, 33, 35, 35) 38 sts, bind off 20 (20, 23, 25, 25) 28 sts, continue across rem 10 sts.

Next row: Work to bound-off sts, slip sts from pocket liner to left needle, knit them, and continue across row.

Continue with decreases as established. **At the same time**, work a buttonhole every 3 (3, 3, 3¼, 3¼) 3½ in. / 7.5 (7.5, 7.5, 8, 8) 9 cm as follows:

Next row (RS): Sl1, k4, bind off 3 sts, continue across row.

Next row: Work as established, cast on 3 sts over bound-off sts.

Repeat last 2 rows for each buttonhole.

When piece measures approx. 13 (14½, 14½, 15½, 17) 17½ in. / 33 (37, 37, 39.5, 43) 44.5 cm from beginning, continue with buttonholes and work shaping as follows:

Waist to Bust Shaping (Continue with Buttonholes)

To work an increase row on RS: Sl1, knit to last 2 sts, kfb, k1.

To work an increase row on WS: Sl1, kfb, knit to end.

Work an increase row every 8th (8th, 9th, 11th, 11th) 11th row 4 times total to 47 (51, 53, 54, 58) 61 sts. End having completed a RS row.

Armhole Shaping

Note: For ease in measuring depth of armhole, place a hanging marker somewhere in the middle of the first row.

(WS): Bind off 5 sts at the beginning of row, knit to end [42 (46, 48, 49, 53) 56 sts rem].

Next row (RS): Sl1, ssk, knit to end.

Next row (WS): Sl1, knit to end.

Work last 2 rows 4 times more to 37 (41, 43, 44, 48) 51 sts.

When armhole measures 3½ (4, 4, 4½, 4½) 4½ in. / 9 (10, 10, 11.5, 11.5) 11.5 cm, end having completed a WS row.

Increase row (RS): Sl1, work to last 2 sts, kfb, k1.

Work an increase row every 8th row 4 times more to 42 (46, 48, 49, 53) 56 sts.

Continue on these sts (if necessary) until total length of armhole measures 6 (6½, 7, 7½, 7½) 8 in. / 15 (16.5, 18, 19, 19) 20.5 cm. End having completed a WS row.

Front Neck Shaping

(RS): Bind off 13 (13, 14, 14, 15) 15 sts, knit next 12 (15, 15, 15, 16) 16 sts [13 (16, 16, 16, 17) 17 sts on needle] and place on a holder or waste yarn, and knit across rem 16 (17, 18, 19, 21) 24 sts.

Row 1 (WS): Sl1, knit to last 3 sts, k2tog, k1.

Row 2 (RS): Sl1, knit across.

Work Rows 1 and 2 twice more, then work Row 1.

Shoulder Shaping

Next row (RS): Sl1, knit to last 2 (2, 2, 2, 3) 3 sts, w&t. Work back.

Next row (RS): Sl1, knit to last 4 (4, 4, 4, 6) 6 sts, w&t. Work back.

Next row (RS): Sl1, knit to last 6 (6, 6, 6, 9) 9 sts, w&t. Work back.

Next row (RS): Sl1, knit to last 8 (8, 8, 8, 12) 12 sts, w&t. Work back.

Next row (RS): Sl1, knit to last 10 (10, 10, 10, 15) 15 sts, w&t. Work back.

Next row (RS): Sl1, knit to last 12 (12, 12, 12, 18) 18 sts, w&t. Work back.

Work one more row and pick up wraps (place on left needle and knit together with next st). Turn work to WS and use the three-needle bind-off (see page 117) to connect shoulders together.

COLLAR

Place all live sts on a needle. Join new yarn and knit around, picking up stitch for stitch on edges of neck shaping. On next row, decrease sts evenly around on back sts and neck shaping (leave front sts as set) to 82 (84, 86, 88, 90) 94 sts.

Slip the first st of every row and work until collar measures 3½ (3½, 3½, 4, 4) 4 in. / 7.5 (7.5, 7.5, 10, 10) 10 cm. Bind off.

SLEEVES (make two)

At underarm, from RS place a marker after first and before last 5 sts; join yarn and pick up and knit 70 (76, 80, 86, 86) 90 sts around armhole edge between markers.

Next row (WS): Sl1, knit to last st, slip last st to right needle, then pick up bound-off st from underarm and place on left needle. Put slipped st back to left needle and knit it together with bound-off st.

Repeat last row until all bound-off sts are worked into sleeve.

Work 11 (9, 9, 7, 8) 7 rows.

Decrease row: Sl1, ssk, knit to last 3 sts, k2tog, k1.

Work a decrease row every 12th (10th, 10th, 8th, 9th) 8th row 12 (15, 16, 19, 18) 20 times total [46 (46, 48, 48, 50) 50 sts rem].

Work even if necessary until sleeve from underarm measures 14½ (15, 15½, 16, 16½) 17 in. / 37 (38, 39.5, 40.5, 42) 43 cm, or desired length. Bind off using the I-cord bind-off (see page 117 for instructions).

POCKET FLAPS (make two)

Cast on 23 (23, 26, 28, 28) 31 sts.

Row 1: Sl1, knit across.

Repeat Row 1 until flap measures 2 in. / 5 cm (or desired width) and finish with I-cord bind-off. At end of row, turn work clockwise and continue with attached I-cord around the finished edges.

When 3 sts rem, graft to beginning of cord, leaving a tail for sewing to top of pocket opening.

BACK BELT (make one)

Cast on 30 (32, 33, 34, 35) 36 sts.

Row 1: Sl1, knit across.

Repeat Row 1 until belt measures 2 in. / 5 cm (or desired width) and finish with I-cord bind-off. At end of row, turn work clockwise and continue with attached I-cord around the finished edges.

FINISHING

Stitch down pocket liners to inside.

Sew pocket flaps from RS to top of pocket openings.

Sew side and underarm seams from the RS using a whipstitch into each chained edge st.

Stitch belt at back waist area. Sew on two decorative buttons.

Sew five buttons opposite buttonholes, and five corresponding on other front.

Weave in all ends and steam lightly or block according to directions on ball band.

From the RS, beginning at bottom side edge (or desired place), work attached I-cord edging around entire coat. Graft or join I-cord ends together and weave in ends.

tweed poncho

Oversized, warm, cuddly, and cabled, this piece works up quickly with large needles and two strands of yarn held together. Omit sleeves for a more blanket-type poncho.

SIZES

All Girls sizes 6/7 (8/9, 10/12)

Instructions are written for size 6/7; all other sizes are in parentheses.

FINISHED MEASUREMENTS

Width: 28 (31, 34) in. / 71 (78.5, 86.5) cm
Length from neck: 21 (24, 27) in. / 53.5 (61, 68.5) cm

YARN

Lion Brand Yarn Vanna's Choice; 3 oz. / 85 g each
    approx. 145 yd. / 133 m; 92% acrylic, 8% rayon
    • 12 (14, 16) skeins #403 Barley

MATERIALS

    • Size US 15 / 10 mm 29 or 36 in. / 73.5 or 91.5 cm
      circular needle
    • Size US 11 / 8 mm 16 in. / 40.5 cm circular needle
    • Tapestry needle
    • Waste yarn
    • Stitch markers

GAUGE

8 sts and 16 rows to 4 in. / 10 cm in St st with two strands
    held together on size US 15 / 10 mm needles

STITCH GUIDE

C4B. Slip next 2 sts and hold at back, k2, then k2 from CN.

C4F. Slip next 2 sts and hold at front, k2, then k2 from CN.

C6B. Slip next 3 sts and hold at back, k3, then k3 from CN.

C6F. Slip next 3 sts and hold at front, k3, then k3 from CN.

T4B. Slip next 2 sts and hold at back, k2, then p2 from CN.

T4F. Slip next 2 sts and hold at front, p2, then k2 from CN.

FRONT CENTER CABLE (over 30 sts)

Row 1 (RS): K9, C6B, C6F, k9.
Row 2 and all WS rows: P30.
Row 3: K6, C6B, k6, C6F, k6.
Row 5: K3, C6B, k12, C6F, k3.

Row 7: C6B, k18, C6F.
Row 8: Same as Row 2.
Repeat Rows 1–8 for pattern.

LATTICE CABLE (multiple of 8 + 10)

Row 1 (RS): P3, C4B, *p4, C4B, repeat from * to last 3 st, p3.
Row 2 and all WS rows: Knit the knits and purl the purls.
Row 3: P1, *T4B, T4F, repeat from * to last st, p1.
Row 5: P1, k2, p4, *C4F, p4, repeat from * to last 3 sts, k2, p1.
Row 7: P1, *T4F, T4B, repeat from * to last 3 sts, k2, p1.
Row 8: Same as Row 2.
Repeat these 8 rows for pattern.

PATTERN NOTE

- Entire garment is made with two strands of yarn held together.

FRONT AND BACK

Note: Before beginning, pull out two 36 in. / 91.5 cm lengths of yarn and set aside for neck shaping later.

With two strands held together, cast on 112 (118, 124) sts.

Row 1 (RS): K2, work Row 1 of Lattice Cable over next 34 sts, k1, p4 (7, 10), work Row 1 of Front Center Cable over next 30 sts, p4 (7, 10), k1, work Row 1 of Lattice Cable over next 34 sts, k2.

Row 2: P2, work Row 2 of Lattice Cable over next 34 sts, p1, k4 (7, 10), work Row 2 of Front Center Cable over next 30 sts, k4 (7, 10), p1, work Row 2 of Lattice Cable over next 34 sts, p2.

These 2 rows set pattern.

Continue with pattern until piece measures approx. 21 (24, 27) in. / 53.5 (61, 68.5) cm (or desired length from neck). End having completed Row 1 of cable patterns.

Row 2 (WS): Work to center cable, bind off 30 sts and continue in pattern across row.

Row 3: Working on these sts only, work to last 2 sts, p2tog.

Row 4: Work across as established.

Row 5: Work to end of row (do not cut yarn; you'll return to these sts after working other side).

Join saved yarn at neck edge on RS and, beginning with Row 3 of pattern, work as follows:

Row 3 (RS): P2tog, work across.

Row 4: Work as established. Cut yarn. (Although only 1 st at each neck edge is decreased, it allows head to better fit through neck opening.)

Return to other needle and with working yarn use the knitted cast-on (see page 117) to cast on 32 sts over bound-off neck and complete Row 5 all the way across [112 (118, 124) sts]. Hang a marker here at both edges for shoulders.

Row 6 (WS): Work as established across all sts.

Note: To keep Center Cable right side up on the back, directions are replaced for Front Center Cable with Back Center Cable (begin on Row 7, then work Rows 1–8 for pattern), as follows:

BACK CENTER CABLE

Row 7 (RS): K9, C6F, C6B, k9.
Row 8: P30.
Row 1 (RS): C6F, k18, C6B.
Row 2 and all WS rows: P30.
Row 3: K3, C6F, k12, C6B, k3.
Row 5: K6, C6F, k6, C6B, k6.
Repeat Rows 1–8.

Complete back until same length as front and bind off loosely in pattern.

COLLAR

With smaller 16 in. / 40.5 cm needle, begin at center back and pick up and knit 50–54 sts (doesn't have to be exact) around neck opening (work 2 sts together at cable crossing at front and back center). Place a marker at beg of round.
Purl 8 rnds (or desired depth of collar).
Bind off loosely purlwise.

CUFFS (make two)

Fold poncho in half at shoulder marker and mark 6 in. / 15 cm down from shoulder on either side (12 in. / 30.5 cm total). Pick up and knit 31 sts between markers (try k2, skip one).
Next row (WS): Knit.
Next row (RS): Purl.
Work 5 more rows in Reverse St st.
Change to [k1, p1] rib and work 6 rows.

Decrease row (RS): K1, work 2tog (k or p following the pattern of the second stitch being decreased), rib to last 3 sts, work 2tog, k1.

Rib another 6 rows, then work a decrease row once more [27 sts rem].

Continue with no further decreases until cuff measures 5 (7, 9) in. / 12.5 (18, 23) cm, or desired length. Bind off loosely in pattern, leaving a tail long enough to stitch cuff and side seam.

Make second cuff to match.

FINISHING

Stitch cuffs and side seams. Weave in any loose ends.

sporty stripes dress and jacket

The dress is designed in two versions, one with a bit of stranded colorwork on the front and one plain version for those not yet ready to tackle stranded colorwork and stripes at the same time. Make the easy bolero-style jacket to go over either style.

sporty stripes dress

SIZES
Girls 6 (7, 8, 10, 12): Young Juniors 5/6 (7/8, 9/10, 11/12)
Instructions are written for size 6; all other sizes follow.
Girls and Young Juniors sizes are separated with a colon.
For ease in knitting, circle your size before beginning.

FINISHED MEASUREMENTS
Chest: 24 (25, 26, 28, 30): 26 (28, 30, 32) in. / 61 (63.5,
  66, 71, 76): 66 (71, 76, 81.5) cm
Waist: 21 (22, 23, 24, 25): 22 (24, 25, 26) in. / 53.5 (56,
  58.5, 61, 63.5): 56 (61, 63.5, 66) cm
Skirt length from waist: 13 (14, 15, 16½, 17): 14½ (15, 16½,
  17) in. / 33 (35.5, 38, 42, 43): 37 (38, 42, 43) cm

YARN
Cascade Yarns Sunseeker; 3.5 oz. / 100 g each approx.
  237 yd. / 217 m; 47% cotton, 48% acrylic, 5% metallic
  • 1 (1, 1, 2, 2): 2 (2, 3, 3) skeins #03 White (A)
  • 1 (1, 1, 2, 2): 2 (2, 3, 3) skeins #05 Black or
    #06 Red (B)

MATERIALS
  • Size US 4 / 3.5 mm 24 in. / 61 cm circular needle
    (*or size to obtain gauge*)
  • One double-pointed needle in same size for I-cord
  • Tapestry needle (sharp yarn darner works best for
    tucking cotton ends)
  • Waste yarn
  • 2 ring-type markers
  • Crochet hook (if desired) for provisional cast-on
  • Pin-type markers

GAUGE
22 sts and 28 rows to 4 in. / 10 cm in St st

PATTERN NOTES

- The skirt front and back are knitted separately to avoid color jogs where stripes would meet if working in the round. Sleeve edges are picked up and knitted in the round. The entire garment is worked in St st and finished with picked up borders and I-cord bind-off.
- Although any cast-on will work, the provisional cast-on (see page 117) allows for easy pick-up for the I-cord edge from cast-on or side edges.
- Do not cut yarn after each color change, but carry up at opposite side edges. Slide work to other end of needle to pick up colors as needed. Adding the second color from the wrong side distributes the yarn evenly at the sides, eliminating all the carries up one side edge only.
- Follow the same instructions for the black or red version, except at bodice front.

SKIRT FRONT

Using a provisional cast-on and Color A (White), cast on 104 (112, 118, 126, 132): 110 (116, 122, 132) sts. Knit one row.

Add B on RS and knit one row, then purl one row. Slide work to other end and purl one row with A.

On next row, work decrease row as follows with A:

Decrease row (RS): K1, ssk, knit to last 3 sts, k2tog, k1.

Continue changing colors every 2 rows and at the same time, work decrease row every 4th row 22 (24, 26, 28, 29): 23 (25, 26, 29) times more. *Note* If you want a shorter skirt, decrease evenly across row to [58 (62, 64, 68, 72): 62 (64, 68, 72)] sts at any time for the waist. Continue to bodice, having completed a second row of Color A.

Work without further decreases until skirt from beginning measures 13 (14, 15, 16½, 17): 14½ (15, 16½, 17) in. / 33 (35.5, 38, 42, 43): 37 (38, 42, 43) cm or desired length. End having completed a second row of color A.

BODICE FRONT
Black-and-White Patterned Version

(skip ahead for directions for red and white striped version)

Note: Please read ahead; several things are going on at the same time. The central panel will continue with two-row stripes of each color, while the side stitches are worked in Fair Isle. Twist yarns when changing colors to avoid holes. The chart on page 102 is only representative of the pattern. It does not show stitch counts for all sizes or increases, but once the patterning is set for your size, you can use the chart to see how the pattern will develop. Work numbers for your size as follows:

Row 1 (RS): [K2 with B, k2 with A] 4 (4, 4, 5, 5): 4 (4, 5, 5) times, k2 with B, PM, continue with B across center 22 (26, 28, 24, 28): 24 (28, 24, 28) sts, PM, k2 with B, [k2 with A, k2 with B] 4 (4, 4, 4, 5): 4 (4, 5, 5) times.

Row 2: Purl across, keeping same colors as previous row (black over black, white over white).

Continue working center panel between markers in horizontal stripes and sides in vertical stripes. **At the same time,** work increase row every 8th (8th, 8th, 8th, 8th): 8th (6th, 6th, 8th) row 4 (3, 4, 5, 5): 5 (7, 7, 7) times to 66 (68, 72, 78, 82): 72 (78, 82, 86) sts. Increases will remain in color B only (chart does not show increases).

To work an increase row on RS: K1, M1, knit to last st, M1, k1.

BLACK-AND-WHITE PATTERNED BODICE

Color A
Color B

To work an increase row on WS: P1, M1, purl to last st, M1, p1.

At the same time, when section from waist measures 2½ (3, 3½, 4, 4½): 4½ (4½, 5½, 6) in. / 6.5 (7.5, 9, 10, 11.5): 11.5 (11.5, 14, 15) cm, ready to work a Color A (white) stripe through the middle section on the RS, continue with increases (not shown on chart) and work chart Row 63 (for your size) through Row 82 (colorwork complete).

Continue if necessary with stripes and increases until bodice measures 5½ (6, 6½, 7, 7½): 7½ (7½, 8½, 9) in. / 14 (15, 16.5, 18, 19): 19 (19, 21.5, 23) cm from beginning (or desired length to armholes).

BODICE FRONT
Red and White Plain Striped Version

Continue in two-row stripe pattern. **At the same time,** work increase row every 8th (8th, 8th, 8th, 8th): 8th (6th, 6th, 8th) row 4 (3, 4, 5, 5): 5 (7, 7, 7) times to 66 (68, 72, 78, 82): 72 (78, 82, 86) sts.

To work an increase row on RS: K1, M1, knit to last st, M1, k1.

To work an increase row on WS: P1, M1, purl to last st, M1, p1.

Continue with stripes and increases until bodice measures 5½ (6, 6½, 7, 7½): 7½ (7½, 8½, 9) in. / 14 (15, 16.5, 18, 19): 19 (19, 21.5, 23) cm from beginning (or desired length to armholes).

BODICE FRONT CONTINUED
Both Versions

Armhole Shaping

Continue across all sts in two-row horizontal stripes as set.

Row 1 (RS): Bind off 3 (3, 4, 4, 5): 4 (5, 5, 5) sts at the beginning of the next 2 rows. Place a pin-type marker somewhere in the middle of this row for ease in measuring the armhole depth.

Next row (RS): K1, ssk, knit to last 3 sts, k2tog, k1. Purl one row.

Repeat last 2 rows 5 (4, 4, 5, 4): 6 (6, 6, 5) times more to 48 (52, 54, 58, 62): 50 (54, 58, 64) sts.

Work even until armhole depth measures 2½ (3, 3½, 3½, 3½): 3 (3½, 3½, 3½) in. / 6.5 (7.5, 9, 9, 9): 7.5 (9, 9, 9) cm. End having completed a WS row.

Front Neck Shaping

Next row (RS): Work across 33 (37, 39, 41, 46): 35 (39, 41, 46) sts, place last 18 (22, 24, 24, 28): 20 (24, 24, 28) sts *just worked* on a holder or waste yarn for center front neck and continue across 15 (15, 15, 17, 17): 15 (15, 17, 18) sts for right shoulder. Purl back.

Next row, all sizes (RS): K1, ssk, work to end of row.

Next row: Purl.

Repeat last 2 rows 6 times more [8 (8, 8, 10, 10): 8 (8, 10, 11) sts rem].

Continue without further decreases until armhole measures 4½ (5, 5½, 5½, 5½): 5 (5½, 5½, 5½) in. / 11.5 (12.5, 14, 14, 14): 12.5 (14, 14, 14) cm. Place sts on a holder or waste yarn.

Left Shoulder Shaping

Join new yarn at armhole edge.

Next row (RS): Work across to last 3 sts, k2tog, k1.

Next row: Purl.

Repeat last 2 rows 6 times more [8 (8, 8, 10, 10): 8 (8, 10, 11) sts rem].

Continue without further decreases until armhole measures 4½ (5, 5½, 5½, 5½): 5 (5½, 5½, 5½) in. / 11.5 (12.5, 14, 14, 14): 12.5 (14, 14, 14) cm. Place sts on a holder or waste yarn.

SKIRT BACK

Using a provisional cast-on and Color A (White), cast on 104 (112, 118, 126, 132): 110 (116, 122, 132) sts.

Knit one row.

Add B on RS and knit one row, then purl one row.

Slide work to other end and purl one row with A.

On next row, work decrease row as follows with A:

Decrease row (RS): K1, ssk, knit to last 3 sts, k2tog, k1.

Continue changing colors every 2 rows. **At the same time,** work decrease row every 4th row 22 (24, 26, 28, 29): 23 (25, 26, 29) times more to 58 (62, 64, 68, 72): 62 (64, 68, 72) sts, same as for front.

Work without further decreases until skirt from beginning measures 13 (14, 15, 16½, 17): 14½ (15, 16½, 17) in. / 33 (35.5, 38, 42, 43): 37 (38, 42, 43) cm, or desired length. End having completed a second row of Color A.

BODICE BACK

Continue in two-row stripe pattern. **At the same time,** work increase row every 8th (8th, 8th, 8th, 8th): 8th (6th, 6th, 8th) row 4 (3, 4, 5, 5): 5 (7, 7, 7) times to 66 (68, 72, 78, 82): 72 (78, 82, 86) sts.

Increase row on RS: K1, M1, knit to last st, M1, k1.

Increase row on WS: P1, M1, purl to last st, M1, p1.

Continue with stripes and increases until bodice measures 5½ (6, 6½, 7, 7½): 7½ (7½, 8½, 9) in. / 14 (15, 16.5, 18, 19): 19 (19, 21.5, 23) cm from beginning (or desired length to armholes).

Armhole Shaping

Row 1 (RS): Bind off 3 (3, 4, 4, 5): 4 (5, 5, 5) sts at the beginning of the next 2 rows. Place a pin-type marker somewhere in the middle of this row for ease in measuring the armhole depth.

Next row (RS): K1, ssk, knit to last 3 sts, k2tog, k1.

Purl one row.

Repeat last 2 rows 5 (4, 4, 5, 4): 6 (6, 6, 5) times more to 48 (52, 54, 58, 62): 50 (54, 58, 64) sts.

Work even until back measures 1½ in. / 4 cm past the front neck shaping. End having completed a WS row.

Back Neck Shaping

Next row (RS): Work across 34 (38, 40, 42, 46): 36 (40, 42, 47) sts, place last 20 (24, 26, 26, 30): 22 (26, 26, 30) sts *just worked* on a holder or waste yarn for center back neck and continue across 14 (14, 14, 16, 16): 14 (14, 16, 17) sts for right shoulder. Purl back.

Next row, all sizes (RS): K1, ssk, work to end of row.

Next row: Purl.

Repeat last 2 rows 5 times more [8 (8, 8, 10, 10): 8 (8, 10, 11) sts rem].

Continue without further decreases, if necessary, to match length of front. Place sts on a holder or waste yarn.

Left Shoulder Shaping

Join new yarn at armhole edge.

Next row (RS): Work across to last 3 sts, k2tog, k1.

Next row: Purl.

Repeat last 2 rows 5 times more [8 (8, 8, 10, 10): 8 (8, 10, 11) sts rem].

Continue without further decreases same as for right shoulder. Place sts on a holder or waste yarn.

FINISHING

Join shoulders with three-needle bind-off (see page 117) from the WS.

Sew side seams using a mattress stitch from the RS, being careful to line up stripes at the edges.

Beginning at center of underarm, with desired color for I-cord border, pick up and knit 3 out of 4 sts around (you can use your 24 in. / 61 cm needle). Work I-cord bind-off (see page 117).

Repeat for other armhole, neck edge, and around skirt bottom.

Weave in all ends, splitting each stitch on the back with a sharp yarn needle. This will keep them in place.

Steam or block according to directions on ball band.

sporty stripes jacket

SIZES
Girls 6 (7, 8, 10, 12): Young Juniors 5/6 (7/8, 9/10, 11/12)

FINISHED MEASUREMENTS
Chest: 24 (25, 26, 28, 30): 26 (28, 30, 32) in. / 61 (63.5, 66, 71, 76): 66 (71, 76, 81.5) cm

YARN
Cascade Yarns Sunseeker; 3.5 oz. / 100 g each approx. 237 yd. / 217 m; 47% cotton, 48% acrylic, 5% metallic
- 1 skein #05 Black (Girls and Young Juniors size 12 will need slightly more than 1 skein; you should have some left over from dress to complete jacket. Girls size 10 will use all of 1 skein.)

MATERIALS
- Size US 4 / 3.5 mm 24 in. / 61 cm circular needle (*or size to obtain gauge*)
- Tapestry needle (sharp yarn darner works best for tucking cotton ends)
- Waste yarn
- 2 ring-type markers

GAUGE
22 sts and 28 rows to 4 in. / 10 cm in St st

BACK

Cast on 66 (68, 72, 78, 82): 72 (78, 82, 88) sts.

Work in St st for 2½ (2½, 3, 3, 3½): 3 (3½, 3½, 4) in. / 6.5 (6.5, 7.5, 7.5, 9): 7.5 (9, 9, 10) cm or desired length to armhole. End having completed a WS row.

Armhole Shaping

Bind off 6 sts at the beginning of the next 2 rows.

Next row (RS): K1, ssk, knit to last 3 sts, k2tog, k1.

Purl one row.

Repeat last 2 rows 3 times more to 46 (48, 52, 58, 62): 52 (58, 62, 68) sts.

Work even on these sts until armhole measures 4½ (5, 5½ , 5½, 5½): 5 (5½, 5½, 5½) in. / 11.5 (12.5, 14, 14, 14): 12.5 (14, 14, 14) cm from beginning.

Place 13 (14, 15, 16, 16): 15 (16, 18, 18) sts on separate holders or waste yarn for each shoulder and center 20 (24, 22, 26, 30): 22 (26, 26, 32) back neck sts on another holder.

LEFT FRONT

Cast on 25 (27, 29, 31, 33): 29 (32, 34, 36) sts.

Purl first row.

Next row (RS): Knit to last st, M1, k1.

Next row: Purl.

Repeat last 2 rows 7 times more to 33 (35, 37, 39, 41): 37 (40, 42, 44) sts. Continue working even until piece measures 2½ (2½, 3, 3, 3½): 3 (3½, 3½, 4) in. / 6.5 (6.5, 7.5, 7.5, 9): 7.5 (9, 9, 10) cm from beginning. End having completed a WS row.

Armhole Shaping

Bind off 6 sts at the beginning of RS row, knit to end.

Next row: Purl.

Next row: K1, ssk, knit to end.

Repeat last 2 rows 3 times more to 23 (25, 27, 29, 31): 27 (30, 32, 34) sts.

Purl one row.

Neck Shaping

Decrease row (RS): Knit to last 3 sts, k2tog, k1.

Working in St st, work decrease row every other row 10 (11, 12, 13, 15): 12 (14, 14, 16) times total to 13 (14, 15, 16, 16): 15 (16, 18, 18) sts.

Work even if necessary until armhole measures 4½ (5, 5½, 5½, 5½): 5 (5½, 5½, 5½) in. / 11.5 (12.5, 14, 14, 14): 12.5 (14, 14, 14) cm. Place sts on a holder or waste yarn.

RIGHT FRONT

Cast on 25 (27, 29, 31, 33): 29 (32, 34, 36) sts.

Next row: Purl.

Next row (RS): K1, M1, knit to end.

Repeat these 2 rows 7 times more to 33 (35, 37, 39, 41): 37 (40, 42, 44) sts.

Continue working even until piece measures 2½ (2½, 3, 3, 3½): 3 (3½, 3½, 4) in. / 6.5 (6.5, 7.5, 7.5, 9): 7.5 (9, 9, 10) cm from beginning. End having completed a RS row.

Armhole Shaping

Bind off 6 sts at the beginning of WS row, purl to end.

Next row: Knit.

Next row: P1, p2tog, purl to end.

Repeat last 2 rows 3 times more to 23 (25, 27, 29, 31): 27 (30, 32, 34) sts.

Knit one row.

Neck Shaping

Decrease row (WS): Purl to last 3 sts, p2tog-tbl, p1.

Working in St st, work decrease row every other row 10 (11, 12, 13, 15): 12 (14, 14, 16) times total to 13 (14, 15, 16, 16): 15 (16, 18, 18) sts.

Work even if necessary until armhole measures 4½ (5, 5½, 5½, 5½): 5 (5½, 5½, 5½) in. / 11.5 (12.5, 14, 14, 14): 12.5 (14, 14, 14) cm.

Connect the shoulders using the three-needle bind-off (see page 117) from the WS.

SLEEVES

From RS, pick up and knit 3 out of 4 sts from one arm-hole bind-off to the other.

Purl one row.

Next row: Knit to last 4 sts, w&t.

Purl to last 4 sts, w&t.

Knit to last 8 sts, w&t.

Purl to last 8 sts, w&t.

Knit to last 12 sts, w&t.

Purl to last 12 sts, w&t.

Knit to last 16 sts, w&t.

Purl to last 16 sts, w&t.

Knit to last 20 sts, w&t.

Purl to last 20 sts, w&t.

Knit across, picking up wraps as you go (to pick up a wrap on the RS, insert needle into wrap first and then knit it tog with st on left needle).

Purl across, picking up rem wraps (to pick up wraps on a purl side, pick up the wrap from behind with the right needle, place it on the left needle and purl it tog with st on left needle).

Next row (RS): Decrease 6 (6, 8, 8, 8): 8 (10, 10, 12) sts evenly across.

Next row (WS): Knit across.

Bind off on RS.

Sew side and underarm seams with a mattress stitch from RS.

BORDER

From the RS, begin at either side seam and pick up all sts around entire border, including live sts from center back.

(WS): Knit one row.

Bind off loosely on RS.

FINISHING

Weave in all ends and steam lightly or block according to directions on ball band.

hawaii dress

An intarsia lover's dream, this multicolored skirt is fashioned after a Kaffe Fassett classic. The bodice gives you a break, and the top is finished with a no-shaping boatneck. Front and back are the same, with minimal shaping through the solid area of the bodice.

SIZES
Girls 6 (7, 8, 10, 12): Young Juniors 5/6 (7/8, 9/10, 11/12)
Instructions are written for size 6; all other sizes follow. Girls and Young Juniors sizes are separated with a colon. For ease in knitting, circle your size before beginning.

FINISHED MEASUREMENTS
Chest: 24 (25, 26, 28, 30): 26 (28, 30, 32) in. / 61 (63.5, 66, 71, 76): 66 (71, 76, 81.5) cm
Waist: 21 (22, 23, 24½, 25½): 22½ (24, 25, 26) in. / 53.5 (56, 58.5, 62, 65): 57 (61, 63.5, 66) cm
Skirt length from dropped waist: 11 (12, 12½, 12½, 13): 12½ (13, 14, 14½) in. / 28 (30.5, 32, 32, 33): 32 (33, 35.5, 37) cm
Total length: 21 (22, 23, 25, 27): 22½ (23½, 25½, 27½) in. / 53.5 (56, 58.5, 63.5, 68.5): 57 (59.5, 65, 70) cm

YARN
Hanalei Hand-Dyed Cotton/Bamboo; 3.5 oz. / 100 g each 400 yd. / 440 m
- 2 skeins (all sizes) Natural
- 1 skein (all sizes) each Rainbow, Blue, Pink, Yellow, Green, and Purple

MATERIALS
- Size US 2 / 2.75 mm 24 in. / 61 cm (or longer) circular needle (*or size to obtain gauge*)
- Size US 2 / 2.75 mm 16 in. / 40.5 cm circular needle (for neck opening)
- Tapestry needle
- Sharp yarn darner
- 4 pin-type markers
- Ring-type markers

GAUGE
32 sts and 40 rows to 4 in. / 10 cm in St st

109

STITCH GUIDE

M1P. Lift bar between sts from the back and purl into the front of it.

PATTERN NOTES

- The front and back are worked separately.
- For this intarsia pattern, cut long lengths of yarn, and when everything tangles into the jumble it will, you can easily pull the yarns through the pile. With this method, very few knots will impede your progress.
- A sharp yarn darner is a must for splitting sts while tucking in ends.

FRONT

With Natural, cast on 230 (240, 240, 248, 256): 240 (240, 248, 256) sts. Work in St st (knit on RS, purl on WS) for 1½ in. / 4 cm.

Using chart on page 111 as a guide, follow chart sequence: *Yellow, Blue, Rainbow, Purple, Green, Pink; repeat from *, working 6 sts in each color across (or set your own color and/or stripe sequence). Knit any remaining sts in the next color in sequence.

Each consecutive row moves over one st. Work 16 rows. On Row 17, change direction.

Continue following chart as established, changing direction every 16th row until skirt from the beginning measures 11½ (12, 12½, 13½, 14½): 12½ (13½, 14½, 15½) in. / 29 (30.5, 32, 34.5, 37): 32 (34.5, 37, 39.5) cm or desired length to waist. End having completed a WS row.

HAWAII DRESS CHART

Yellow
Blue
Rainbow
Purple
Green
Pink

Note: Work the next decrease row in colors to keep pattern.

Next row (RS):

Size 6: K1, *k2tog, k3tog, k3tog; repeat from * to last st, k1 [86 sts rem].

Size 7: *K2tog, k3tog, k3tog; repeat from * to end [90 sts rem].

Size 8: *K2tog, k3tog; repeat from * to end [96 sts rem].

Size 10: K1,*k2tog, k3tog; repeat from * to last st, k1 [100 sts rem].

Size 12: K1,*k2tog, k3tog; repeat from * to last st, k1 [104 sts rem].

Young jrs. size 5/6: *K2tog, k3tog, k3tog; repeat from * to end [90 sts rem].

Young jrs. size 7/8: *K2tog, k3tog, k3tog; repeat from * to end [96 sts rem].

Young jrs. size 9/10: K1, *k2tog, k3tog; repeat from * to last st, k1 [100 sts rem].

Young jrs. size 11/12: K1, *k2tog, k3tog; repeat from * to last st, k1 [104 sts rem].

Cut all ends leaving tails long enough for tucking.

Bodice

Join Natural on RS and work in St st for 9 (9, 9, 9, 8): 6 (6, 4, 4) rows.

To work an increase row on RS: K1, M1, knit to last st, M1, k1.

To work an increase row on WS: P1, M1P, purl to last st, M1P, p1.

Work an increase row every 10th (10th, 10th, 10th, 9th): 7th (7th, 5th, 5th) row 4 (4, 4, 5, 6): 6 (7, 9, 11) times more to 96 (100, 106, 112, 120): 104 (112, 120, 128) sts.

Continue with no further increases until bodice measures 5 (5, 5, 6, 6½): 5 (5½, 5½, 6) in. / 12.5 (12.5, 12.5, 15, 16.5): 12.5 (14, 14, 15) cm or desired length to armhole. End having completed a WS row.

Mark side edges for armhole placement (very important) and continue with new increases as follows:

Row 1 (RS): K1, M1, knit to last st, M1, k1.

Row 2: Purl across.

Repeat last 2 rows, increasing one st each side every RS row.

When work measures 2½ (2½, 3, 3, 3½): 2½ (2½, 3, 3½) in. / 6.5 (6.5, 7.5, 7.5, 9): 6.5 (6.5, 7.5, 9) cm, cut Natural.

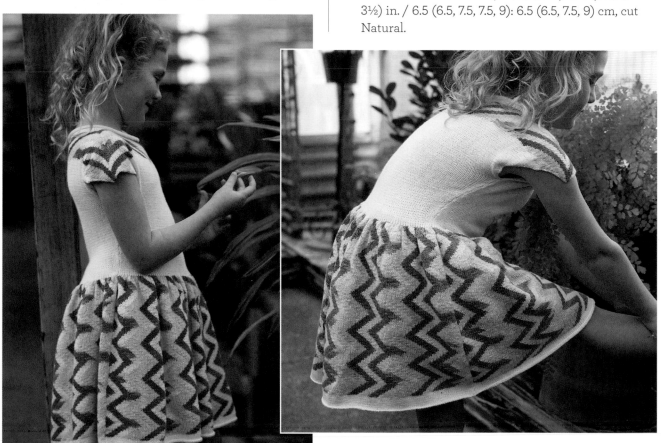

Before continuing, locate center front and mark with a ring-type marker. Count back toward beginning of row in increments of 6 to know where to place (and how many sts for) first colored stripe. See chart on page 114 for center detail (not all sts are depicted). Each row moves one stitch to the right or left as shown.

Continue with increases until 26 rows of chart are complete, approx. 2½ in. / 6.5 cm and 146 (150, 154, 162, 170): 154 (162, 170, 178) sts, or continue working chart and increases if longer sleeve depth is desired. End having completed a WS row. Keep yarns attached and place all sts on a holder or waste yarn.

BACK

Work same as for front. Place all sts on a holder or waste yarn.

SHOULDERS/SLEEVES

On front and back, mark center 68 (68, 72, 72, 80): 68 (72, 76, 80) sts for center neck opening and place markers. Count rem sts for each side and adjust markers so same amount of sts are on each side for shoulder/sleeve (better to have a few extra at neck opening). Use the three-needle bind-off (see page 117) to connect these sts together from the WS using color tails as established.

Repeat for other shoulder/sleeve.

NECK EDGE

From the RS, with Natural, begin at side of neck edge and knit all rem sts around. Continue knitting in the round until collar measures 1 in. / 2.5 cm or desired length. Bind off very loosely.

FINISHING

Sew side seams to armhole markers. Weave in all ends and steam lightly.

CENTER FRONT

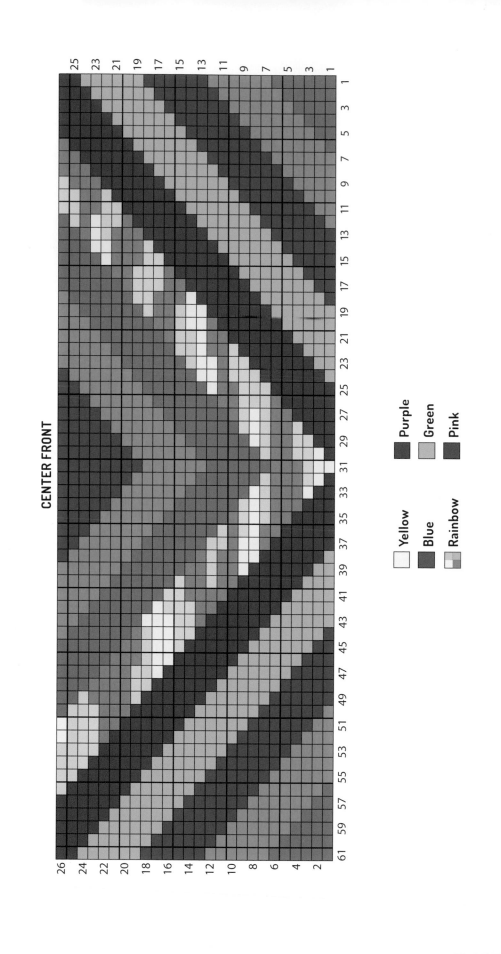

Yellow   Purple

Blue   Green

Rainbow   Pink

approx.	approximately
beg	begin(ning)
CN	cable needle
k	knit
k1b	knit one through the back loop
k2tog	knit 2 stitches together
k3tog	knit 3 stitches together
kfb	knit into the front and back of the same stitch
M1	make 1 lifted increase; lift the horizontal bar between the stitch just worked and the next one from the front and put it on the left needle, then knit (or purl) into the back of it
M1P	make 1 purl
MC	main color
p	purl
p1b	purl one through the back loop
p2tog-tbl	purl 2 stitches together through the back loop
PM	place marker
rem	remain(s, ing)
rnd(s)	round(s)
RS	right side
sl	slip
SM	slip marker

(continued)

ssk	slip 2 stitches (one at a time, knitwise) from the left needle to the right, then knit these 2 stitches together with tip of left needle inserted from left to right into the front of stitches
St st	stockinette stitch; when working back and forth in rows, knit all RS stitches and purl all WS stitches; when working in the round, knit all stitches
st(s)	stitch(es)
tbl	through back loop
w&t	wrap and turn; slip the next stitch, bring the yarn in front, then put the stitch back on the left needle and turn your work to the other side (leaving some stitches unworked). When picking up a wrapped stitch on a right side row, place needle under the wrap first and knit it together with the stitch on needle; when picking up a wrap on the wrong side, pick up the wrap from behind and place on needle, then purl it together with stitch on needle.
WS	wrong side
YO	yarn over

CABLE STITCHES

C4B	slip next 2 sts and hold at back, k2, then k2 from cable needle
C4F	slip next 2 sts and hold at front, k2, then k2 from cable needle
C6B	slip next 3 sts and hold at back, k3, then k3 from cable needle
C6F	slip next 3 sts and hold at front, k3, then k3 from cable needle
T3B	slip next st to CN and hold at back, k2, p1 from CN
T3F	slip next 2 sts to CN and hold at front, p1, k2 from CN
T4B	slip next 2 sts and hold at back, k2, then p2 from cable needle
T4F	slip next 2 sts and hold at front, p2, then k2 from cable needle
T5BP	slip next 3 sts to CN and hold at back, k2, then p1, k2 from CN

Provisional Cast-on

With waste yarn and crochet hook, chain desired number of stitches plus a few more and finish off. Pick up and knit stitches through the back loop of the chain. For those who don't want to crochet, cast on desired number of stitches and knit a few rows in waste yarn before continuing.

Knitted Cast-on

Start with a slipknot (or live stitch) on the left-hand needle. Work a knit stitch with the right-hand needle, but do not slip it off the left needle. Instead, place the loop from the right needle back onto the left needle (one stitch cast on). Continue until the desired number of stitches are on the left needle.

I–cord Cast-on

Cast on 3 sts, slip one st a time to left needle (working yarn remains behind at all times). *Kfb, k2; slip 3 (knitwise) one at a time to left needle; repeat from * until number of stitches needed plus 2. **Next row:** K2tog, k1, slip sts to left needle and knit last 2 together. The I-cord is complete.

I-cord Bind-off from Live Sts

Cast on 3 sts using the knitted cast-on; slip to left needle, *k2, ssk, slip sts back to left needle (do not turn work, carry yarn behind); repeat from *. When 3 sts remain, graft to the beginning of the cord and weave in ends.

Attached I-cord from Cast-on or Side Edges

From RS, pick up and knit one edge stitch and slip to left needle. Cast on 2 more sts with the knitted cast-on; *k2, slip next st, then pick up one st from edge and ssk (do not turn work), slip 3 sts to left needle; repeat from * around. When 3 sts remain, graft to the beginning of the cord and weave in ends.

Three-needle Bind-off

Turn pieces inside out and place live stitches on 2 parallel needles. Then knit 2 stitches together, one from each of the parallel needles. Knit another 2 stitches together, one from each needle. You now have 2 stitches on your right needle; use your left needle to pull the first stitch over the second and off the needle (one stitch bound off). Continue binding off in this manner (k2tog, bind off one).

yarn sources

Berroco
berroco.com

Brown Sheep Company
brownsheep.com

Cascade Yarns
cascadeyarns.com

Ella Rae
https://knittingfever.com/brand/ella-rae

Hanalei Hand-Dyed
hanaleihanddyed.com

Knit Picks
knitpicks.com

Lion Brand
lionbrand.com

Premier Yarns
premieryarns.com